MW01443350

Christian Inversion of Jewish Nationalist Monotheism

Christian Inversion of Jewish Nationalist Monotheism:

Clawing Our Way Back

By

Patrick Madigan

Cambridge
Scholars
Publishing

Christian Inversion of Jewish Nationalist Monotheism:
Clawing Our Way Back

By Patrick Madigan

This book first published 2025

Cambridge Scholars Publishing

Lady Stephenson Library, Newcastle upon Tyne, NE6 2PA, UK

British Library Cataloguing in Publication Data
A catalogue record for this book is available from the British Library

Copyright © 2025 by Patrick Madigan

All rights for this book reserved. No part of this book may be reproduced, stored in a retrieval system, or transmitted, in any form or by any means, electronic, mechanical, photocopying, recording or otherwise, without the prior permission of the copyright owner.

ISBN: 978-1-0364-4051-0
ISBN (Ebook): 978-1-0364-4052-7

TABLE OF CONTENTS

Introduction 1

Chapter 1 3
Christian Inversion of Jewish Nationalist Monotheism, and Its Romantic, Revolutionary and Narcissist Corruptions

Chapter 2 13
From Fusion to Divorce: The Reversal between Classical and Modern Overtures towards the Divine

Chapter 3 21
Proportionate Love and Literature: The Revenge of the Bastard

Chapter 4 27
Apocalypto, The Explosion/Debunking of the 'Noble Savage', and with it of Enlightenment Ethics

Chapter 5 33
The Devil Made Me Do It: How the West Disguised its Diabolical Switch of Messiah

Chapter 6 63
The Sorrow That Dares Not Say Its Name; The Inadequate Father, the Motor of History

Chapter 7 83
Christianity and the Death Penalty

Chapter 8 93
The Supremacy of God and the Love Within God

Chapter 9 99
Clawing Our Way Back; Towards an Ever-Deeper Intervention

INTRODUCTION

During my 16-year service as editor of the *Heythrop Journal*, I reviewed many books and wrote several articles. In retirement, I have had occasion to read through these again and been struck by how a selection could be arranged in a sequence such that the reviews would enter into a 'discussion' and mutually 'pollinate' one another in the reader's mind, such that the resulting experience would be educational, stimulating and satisfying. Beginning with contemporary biblical criticism, I uncover how the Jews, resenting being a 'small' nation, 'backed into' monotheism for primarily political reasons, as a way to argue that their god was distinct and different from the gods of other nations (who followed the 'family of the gods' model or pantheon). This 'one god' with whom they had a special relationship was only punishing them through military defeat for dallying with the other's religion. Thus, in spite of their small size and inglorious military history, they really were superior.

Later, when the Romans destroyed their temple and excluded them from Jerusalem, threatening to wipe them out entirely, some Jews sought comfort and psychological compensation through the postulate of a special 'gnosis' or 'knowledge' supplied them by a 'savior' behind their creator god, that 'lifted them up' and restored a basis for their exceptionalism and superior status. To a now 'converted' or Christian western society the Jews came across as stubbornly 'stiff-necked', defensively haughty and 'different'. They were tolerated because they performed an essential job that no one else could or would do—money lending - but often were treated as a scapegoat whenever tragedy or disaster struck. Jews were banished from England from 1290 to 1657, from France periodically after 1306, and from Spain for several hundred years after the unification of Aragon and Castile in 1492. The two-beat syncopation of rejection or exclusion, followed by psychological compensation, reappeared during the Renaissance in Jewish 'Kabbalah' in Mediterranean Europe in which powerful esoteric predictions were hinted, shortly thereafter by Spinoza with his scandalous 'atheistic' doctrine of universal determinism, and later by Freud with his shocking prescription of infantile sexuality. The most powerful Jewish 'blasphemy' during modernity has been the Marxist criticism of Enlightenment self-centredness, and the adequacy of capitalism as a resulting complete, adult or mature social philosophy, able to construct and deliver a fittingly human, vibrant - and compassionate - social reality without deeper theological support. In a 'closed' world where they often had no rights or were made to move with only what they could carry, the Jews agreed to play the only 'role' on offer. They were perpetually available as everybody's 'victim', but they exacted the psychological compensation of awe and fear as possessing special knowledge or power, which went along with and flattered in a backhanded way their self-estimate. Both sides got what they could live with, if not all they wanted. This continued until the 'final solution', when the roles became exaggerated and the syncopation fell apart.

In the move from the classical to the modern period, three mutually succeeding 'arcs' can be discerned: from reason to scepticism (with Descartes), from freedom to determinism (with Spinoza and Newton) and from annihilation to divinization (with Hegel and Nietzsche). Each one feeds into the next. With the emergence of 'expressive individualism' as the default ethic of our time, we assist at an experiment to see whether long-term civil, cultural and political society is still possible.

Chapter 1

Christian Inversion of Jewish Nationalist Monotheism, and Its Romantic, Revolutionary and Narcissist Corruptions

It is important to see Christianity as an internal reform of Judaism that surprisingly came to overtake its parent and attain independent existence. With the attack on all expressions of transcendence during the Enlightenment, this reform flipped into the enemy that, if it could not be expunged, at least should be flattened and institutionalized, along with its antiquated parent, if society is to free itself from unpredictable and scurrilous outbreaks of this nefarious if apparently inveterate tendency and tropism within human nature, to soar instead into the sunny uplands of a neutralized social reality liberated from superstition and a consequently calmer public space. It is therefore disappointing to discover that, when spurs to internal conflict emanating from rival religious world views or mythic traditions have been eliminated, the human psyche is not finally set free from internal turmoil and incitement to external violence, but depressingly discovers itself at the mercy of a heightened internal sensitivity to accusations of irremediable reproach and eternal inadequacy, an awareness of social barriers that appear impossible to cross, of "prizes" that cannot be captured, which replace the earlier confessional denunciations and expulsions. This heightened social sensitivity, highlighted by Rousseau and recently expanded and richly developed by René Girard, suggests that unless disciplined and corrected—that is, not "left alone"—the human psyche will not return to "psychic health" and attain "secular bliss", but rather becomes vulnerable to lower sources of intimidation and inadequacy; it can even become traumatized, psychotic or bestial from awareness of ordinary social differences. Otherwise, such developments as "serial killing"—puzzling and yet distinctive of our era—become difficult to account for. The U.S. has ten times as many homicides a year as Canada, and over one hundred times as many as the U.K. Also, the U.S. has more serial killings per year than the next six countries combined.

Beginning with contemporary biblical criticism, I uncover how the Jews, resenting being a "small" nation, "backed into" monotheism for primarily political reasons, as a way to argue that their god was distinct and different from the gods of other nations (who followed the "family of the gods" model or pantheon). This "one god" with whom they had a special relationship was only punishing them through military defeat and exile for dallying with the other's religion. Thus, in spite of their small size and inglorious military history, they really were superior (Bonn, 2014).

After the Egyptians declined the monotheistic reform of their religion by the pharaoh Akhenaten, by some means the Jews next door managed to pick up the latter, put the same doctrines into the mouth of their national prophet Moses and imagine that this distinction and unique privilege compensated for their small size, unimpressive natural resources and nonexistent international reputation. Indeed, against all appearances, it lifted them up and constituted them as superior to all other peoples. It gave them a vocation and focus in the direction of political independence and the construction of a temple where the special relationship or covenant between the one deity and the Jewish people could expand into the legal separation, cultic elaboration and theological doctrines that constitute the glory of the Jewish nation and their special gift to less fortunate peoples.

Unfortunately, power politics and international relations proved deaf to this theological script. The Jews were condemned to stay a "buffer state" between nations that possessed superior natural resources such as the Nile River or the Tigris-Euphrates complex. The Jews' awkward, ambiguous visit to Egypt and ignominious departure (despite their compensatory imaginary "victory" at the "Reed" sea) was followed by the loss of the northern kingdom to Assyria and eventually of the southern kingdom to Babylon. Alexander's victory over the Near East changed everything—and he did not even visit—let alone "conquer" Jerusalem!

Actually, there is no explicit assertion of monotheism in the Jewish scriptures before *Second Isaiah,* as the Jews prepare to return to Israel from

Babylon. Once this author had propounded it, it was then 'read back into' the 'henotheism' that characterized the earlier scriptures (each people had its own god, as the Jews had their own, who properly received their worship and cared for them), but it had not originally been there. 'Earlier' books were thus written 'late'—at the end rather than at the beginning. *Genesis*, for example, was written no earlier than just before, and probably during, the Babylonian Exile. Indeed, much of the Old Testament was written in Babylon; it was written in Hebrew, but written *in* Babylon. The Hebrews felt they had to give an account of thèir origins and history that could compete with and rival that of the Babylonians, and later of the Greeks in Alexandria. Monotheism was thus a daring compensation mechanism employed to gain an upper hand over cultures that appeared more powerful or prestigious; it appears psychologically to have been, initially at least, a way to 'save face' before more established kingdoms, on the basis of which to argue their (implausible or counter-intuitive) superiority. The whole 'Moses sequence', for example, was composed to demonstrate the Jews' superiority over the Egyptians, reinforcing both the emerging monotheism and the exclusivity of the Jewish covenant.

This mechanism was not very successful, however. Rather than drawing other nations into their orbit, after their return from Babylon, Jews found themselves more a satellite of the Hellenistic kingdom centered in the "new" capital of Alexandria. The majority of the Jews in Babylonia had not come back, and now even in Jerusalem and Israel generally Jews found themselves speaking Greek! They commissioned a translation of their scriptures into Greek and realized they must now position themselves and make their way in an international, Greek-speaking world where they were not the center but rather an "uppity" protuberance that engaged in pathetic maneuverings to contest the supremacy of Hellenistic culture by whispering, for example, that Greek philosophers had derived their wisdom from Moses. Their "supremacy" and social separation was now leading to their ostracization, irrelevance and detestation by the international community.

The replacement of the Greeks by the Romans only made things worse. The Romans did not feel culturally equal to the Greeks; their skill was administration and discipline. Consequently the Romans did not found independent "Hellenistic kingdoms" around the Mediterranean, but only "outposts" of the single Empire—and they took a dim view of local rebellion. The Romans also felt themselves as an inferior in a "catch-up" competition with Greek culture—the same position the Jews imagined themselves in. The two discovered themselves unpleasantly to be "mirror images" of one another, and they did not like what they saw. They became mortal enemies, both aspiring to the same crown; neither would give in. The Mediterranean stage was set for a tragedy of unprecedented proportions.

Jesus was indifferent to the Jewish-Roman rivalry, but his movement is significant in that it was seen as opening a bridge between Jew and Gentile, cutting off the separation, pretensions and snobbery of the former while opening a portal for Gentiles to share in the privileges and taste the intimacy of those admitted to the special relationship Jews claimed with the single God. Also, Jesus spoke Greek, and the Pauline letters and gospels were all written in Greek.

If anything, Jesus was an 'anti-messianic' figure, claiming that God would not send another David-like figure to establish by conquest another Jewish state on the order of Assyria, Egypt or Babylon; what God wanted was rather an a-political union based on internal conversion and reform. Jesus had not studied the 'Law'; he was not a student of Hillel or Gamaliel, as St. Paul was. He was a disciple only of John the Baptist, but in this radically reversed sense he could be called a 'messiah'. He had preached this new ideal and relationship with the 'Father', which he would invite and also communicate to others. His followers were to become a nation of priests, not of warriors. He had heroically lived the vocation of being the first to reveal this and accepted its consequences. In this striking sense, he could indeed be called the 'messiah', the culminating point, the foundation and goal not only of God's interaction with the Jews, but with all humanity.

Alarmed by the Christian response, the newly-coined rabbis, after the loss of Jerusalem and destruction of the Temple in the Jewish-Roman wars, gradually discouraged Greek translation and removed messianic and apocalyptic (Greek) additions to their scriptures. The "Law" became more prominent in the Gentile identification of the Jew, because after the Roman wars the Jews lost land, king and temple; Law was all they had left of their covenant with the single deity.

Christian Inversion of Jewish Nationalist Monotheism, and Its Romantic, Revolutionary and Narcissist Corruptions

Actually, Jesus seems to have seen himself as the founding-prophet of a new (or final) form of Judaism that would be (following his mentor, John the Baptist) extra-temple and collecting or retrieving the "lost sheep of Israel"—especially those excluded from participation in temple-Judaism because of ritual-purity concerns (i.e., tax collectors and other professions). When challenged by pharisees on intricate questions of the law (a woman is married to seven brothers, all of whom die. Whose wife will she be in the next world?), Jesus showed impatience and exasperation. The heart of religion cannot be concerned with such things. When challenged with how one should behave in a potentially tense situation, again he would typically answer with a parable (the prodigal son, the good Samaritan, etc.), as if to say: "You don't give a hard and fast rule; such would be juvenile and inappropriate. At the same time, the answer is no mystery. Open your heart, and see where the greatest need lies." In other words, the exigency for responsible ethics is still there, but the authorities have misperceived it. The entire super-story of the law must be scrutinized, criticized and largely dismantled; it is a creation of man, not of God. It should be replaced with humility, simplicity and openness. Look at the story of the wealthy pharisee and the poor man who go into the temple together to pray. Only the prayer of the second, who beats his breast, asking for forgiveness, is heard. So what the Jews take pride in—the only thing remaining after the Roman wars, the law—Jesus suggests is a matter for shame. Again, a door is opened to the Gentiles. Later, when a pagan Roman emperor in some desperation began looking about for a new religion to unify his empire to counter the Zoroastrianism of the Persians, Julian "the Apostate" suggested Judaism and bringing back sacrifices; but Constantine had already chosen Christianity. It is difficult to criticize his choice.

Christianity thus came to place its emphasis on transformation of the individual, rather than on incorporation within a group. The distinction is somewhat artificial, as there is little individual transformation that does not take place, especially when we are young, apart from incorporation into a group, whose *mores* or customs we are encouraged to "put on" or adopt, but Christianity was distinctive in forming communities that did not stem from or were made up exclusively of one *ethnos*. It was thus perceived as a novel experiment in world religions, especially by its "parent", Judaism. It provided a way of combining freedom from obligatory compliance with local civic cults while also providing escape and protection from a charge of "atheism", which was regarded as unpatriotic, ungrateful and dangerous.

After their defeat in the Jewish wars, the Romans destroyed their temple and excluded Jews from Jerusalem, threatening to wipe them out entirely. Some Jews sought comfort and psychological compensation through the postulate of a special *"gnosis"* or "knowledge" supplied them by a "savior" behind their creator god, that "lifted them up" and restored a basis for their exceptionalism and superior status. To a now "converted" or Christian western society the Jews came across as "stiff-necked", exotic and defensively haughty. They were tolerated because they performed an essential job that no one else could or would do—money lending—but often were treated as a scapegoat whenever tragedy or disaster struck. The two-beat syncopation of rejection or exclusion, followed by psychological compensation, reappeared during the Renaissance in Jewish "Kabbalah" in Mediterranean Europe in which powerful esoteric predictions were hinted, shortly thereafter by Spinoza with his scandalous "atheistic" doctrine of universal determinism, and later by Freud with his shocking prescription of infantile sexuality. In a "closed" world where they often had no rights or were made to move with only what they could carry, the Jews agreed to play the only "role" on offer. They were perpetually available as everybody's "victim", but they exacted the psychological compensation of awe and fear as possessing special knowledge or power, which went along with and flattered in a back-handed way their self-estimate. Both sides got what they could live with, if not all they wanted. This continued until the "final solution", when the roles became exaggerated and the syncopation fell apart.

Greek philosophers studied the connection between personal moral development and various types of political constitution. The individual was thought of as having an intellect or reason, which should use the will or "spirit" to guide and discipline his passions. The goal of stability for all states was thought of as being shaped by having "wise" people as rulers; with this requirement fulfilled, it was a matter of historical accident or local conditions whether one had one, several or universal suffrage (monarchy, aristocracy or polity). All three were acceptable, but all three could also be corrupted if an improperly formed person seized power (tyranny, oligarchy or democracy). It was practically impossible for anyone to come to moral maturity in the latter states. In the wake of the competition between military generals and the consequent variety of emperors in the late Roman Empire (as well as the variety of leaders in the incoming barbarian tribes as they gradually converted to Christianity), dynasties emerged from noble families to establish monarchy as the most familiar or recognized form of government in the West throughout the Middle Ages, with the king's authority consecrated by the Church, and which reciprocally supported the Church with its cultic and educational institutions. Morality thereby supported politics, and politics reinforced morality.

During the modern period the citizenry has come to lose patience for a variety of reasons with the monarchical form of government. As an experiment, ethnic, social or political "unity" was considered less crucial for the viability of a state; also, monarchy was felt to impede, smother or oppress the unfolding development of its citizens rather than to advance or protect the latter. The "Romantic" movement held that there was a deeper or more important dimension to the individual that could not break to the surface or receive full expression under a monarchical or aristocratic regime. This departure encountered increased irritation in accepting, if only ceremonially, a monarch or aristocrat "over" them. Such negative reaction to their own histories propelled western states into and through a series of revolutions whereby suffrage was extended to all citizens, rendering "democracy" the inevitable, alone acceptable (or "least objectionable") form of restraint upon the interests, opinions and activities of citizens. The challenge was to combine this relaxed license with the order and stability that traditionally had been considered desirable in a state. This change broke the earlier connection between political science and moral development; the state was no longer viewed as the individual "writ large". His "passions" and enthusiasms were no longer necessary to be guided and disciplined by a "spirit" operating under the direction of reason. The active "revolutionary" impulse tolerated, and even encouraged, the liberation, expression and indulgence of tendencies beyond earlier practices. Inevitably concern came to be directed to the question whether this innovation or departure from traditional order between the parts of the psyche was compatible with stability in either the state or the individual. Politics became a tense "juggling act", a precarious and ongoing experiment to discover to what extent and for how long such relaxation could or should be tolerated.

In this last regard, a largely unforeseen experimental transformation took place through the democratic revolution, but it took place "underground", beneath the surface and as a consequence took time to show itself. This was the development, behind the apparently successful, well-rounded, well-adjusted and ordinary or conventional individual, of the psychopathic narcissistic personality, a personality who feels deprived or cheated at some deep but invisible level of the "success" or satisfaction from which others have benefited, and consequently feels he has a "right" to compensation or "pay back" for the setbacks and deprivations he experiences. The "democratic" revolution has given him a hidden anger and concealed resentment at the exceptional "success" others have achieved at his expense; this differential result or shortfall in public acclaim, reward or remuneration, rather than inspiring him to work harder for comparable results, kindles a rageful fire at the embarrassing discrepancy. The indirect "coaching" of democracy, that all are in some fundamental sense "equal", determines him to equalize the situation and obtain what he desires anyway, at all costs—by simply taking it from those who have it, if necessary. The "rights" of others no longer matter to him, he can no longer see himself in the "face" of the other; in fact, he can see no other face but his own. He begins to make an exception of himself—because others have proven themselves no longer able to see him. He feels justified in adopting alternative distractions and forbidden compensations because "society" has not fulfilled its contract with him—to give him adequate response and recognition, equal gratification and appropriate consolation. He is not embarrassed in key situations to covertly put himself first, bulldoze others out of the way and seize the "prize". In cases involving secrecy such psychological reasoning can be used to justify forms of release, compensation, revenge and consolation like insult, vandalism or injury—at its limit, even serial killing. "This is something they have done to me, so I am justified in taking my satisfaction where I discover it." Such behavior is amplified in societies where there is no one dominant group which must be feared or deferred to, so that the individual does not know who to strike out at, or who it is worthwhile to try to join. The individual feels alone. In the USA, the Federal

Bureau of Investigation estimates there are between 30 and 50 serial killers operating at any given time. Their victims are chosen randomly and anonymously; they are strangers. "This is an injury I inflict on 'society', because it is what I deserve."[1] These casualties to extreme alienation are a consequence the democratic revolution did not anticipate and has not as yet developed the psychological resources to help or heal. They are a "flip-side" of the increased empowerment democracy supplies the individual, but also demonstrates that without concomitant education and therapies fostering psychological maturity, such empowerment by itself is dangerous for both the individual and the state.

Note

[1] The scholarly discussion of serial killing is massive and growing. Useful background text is: Scott Bonn, *Why We Love Serial Killers: the Curious Appeal of the World's Savage Murderers*, Skyhorse Press, 2014.

Chapter 2

From Fusion to Divorce: The Reversal between Classical and Modern Overtures towards the Divine

Conventionally we believe that the attitudes of humans towards the divine have always been respectful and positive, but this is not the case. In the early modern period the attitude of some thinkers executed a novel and radical about-face, a hundred-and-eighty degree turn—and this not just towards other humans who continue to harbor warm feelings towards the divine, but towards the deity itself, or at least towards the idea of a single 'monotheistic' deity. They strongly urge a retraction and reversal of the bold and desperate move towards monotheism scholars now believe the Hebrews made late in their history, during the Babylonian captivity, primarily to stave off embarrassment and assimilation into the powerful and sophisticated Persian pantheon. At the time Second Isaiah was prophesying, the Jews quietly and unobtrusively elevated their patronal deity - under a cloud for having failed to protect them from military defeat and cultural humiliation - as not just equal to (or another name for) the Persian high god, but higher still, in fact the unique and only god, who (even more surprisingly) had elected the Hebrews out of all the peoples of the world with whom to contract a covenant of mutual fidelity and support.

In the early modern period it was suggested that this unprecedented, provocative act should be rescinded, recalled and allowed to sink into a dead letter as a disturbance with negative consequences unforeseen at the earlier period but which developed slowly in later history. This step should be retracted, broken off and repudiated, several modern thinkers counsel, not because of the failure of this tribal deity to fulfill his part of the military-political agreement, but rather because of the nefarious effects entertaining the idea of a single metaphysical god has had upon human culture and history, manifest not only in the confusing and conflicting variety of characteristics attributed to him by opposing groups of his followers but primarily due to the stunting, inhibitory, infantilizing and disempowering effect such an allegiance exercises upon societal and individual development. Rather than aspiring towards fusion and participation with this theological fantasy, society should reverse direction, discourage, divorce and forswear this union, cutting away this unhealthy belief as an anchor and drag that has too long held us down and back, so that we can advance proudly to embrace the benefits of newly liberated and freely operating human ingenuity and insight, to carry us to the less dramatic or juvenile but better grounded adult satisfactions of this worldly science. This reconsideration and reversal is already apparent in the superficially devotional poem *Paradise Lost* by John Milton, published in 1667, but stands out more fully fifty years later in the poetic and artistic production of his enthusiastic follower, William Blake. These two announce a new *eschaton* or teleology to both individual and societal development that takes back, cancels and repudiates the previous *eschaton* as a misstep leading unawares to cultural slavery to poorly understood and disempowering dogmas and the abandonment of individual development - substituting a *grand guignol* interpretation and inverse parody of this traditionally proper ambition, and a blasphemous denial of the most basic assumptions upon which cultural advance in the West had been conceived and measured. Milton had to carefully limit the expression of his animus, to discipline and cover the depth of his critique, in order to get his poem past the censor; Blake was put down as an irascible, off-balance social misfit who received private, idiosyncratic revelations, but then dismissed with a shrug as harmless.

The influence and power of the first monotheistic paradigms is not difficult to point out. The repeated attempt by Greek thinkers to unify the contrasting approaches of Plato and Aristotle resulted in the Neo-Platonic 'Great Chain of Being', made famous by Arthur Lovejoy in his book of the same name, which illustrates the scope, malleability and increasing sophistication of this paradigm not only during the classical period (called by Leibniz the 'perennial philosophy'), but reaching far into modernity in scientific and evolutionary circles. So powerful was its intellectual dominance that the latter could mask apparent exceptions to its basic postulates—for example, 'Gnostic' philosophy which began perhaps as a religious heresy within Judaism after the latter's crushing defeats by Roman legions, which led some diaspora Jews to turn against and vilify their 'creator' God as an evil, angry and vengeful demon, to the benefit of a newly-conceived higher and more beneficent 'savior' deity who, through the gift of a 'knowledge' concerning how they had fallen under the power and control of this lower spirit, allowed them to be rescued, transported back and returned to their original condition as it was before the catastrophe of creation and fall (the two are equivalent). So powerful is the earlier paradigm, however, that it is questionable whether the Gnostic challenge, in spite of its shocking and violent opposition to the 'creator God', escaped being incorporated into a 'higher monotheism'. Gnosticism has a long future in the modern period, as new movements began to re-assess supposed 'high points' of their common past and reinterpret these as disastrous 'falls' into corruption, error and slavery, from which 'revelation' is meant to provide escape and return to a higher condition. What first complicates and threatens the descent of beneficent creation is subsequently presented as only a brief 'hitch' necessary as a condition within a larger developmental ascent. For Milton and Blake, however, the diagnosis of these nefarious consequences requires an almost unprecedented (except for Spinoza, who was avoided in horror as a notorious and scandalous 'great atheist') move away from the reverence, longing and fusion with the projected god of creation towards separation, departure and divorce. This pattern casts these latter thinkers as prophets imparting a liberating revelation with its accompanying uplift.

Unlike later naturalistic and reductive critics, Milton and Blake cast their criticism in theological or mythological terms and freely invoke the deity. Milton's grandfather Richard Milton had been an ardent Catholic. When his son John Milton senior became a Protestant, Richard disinherited him. John moved to London and made his living as a scrivener, an established and respected service in the pre-Guttenberg era. John prospered and was able to send his son to St. Paul's school, where young John distinguished himself in languages. After studies in Cambridge and travels in Italy, John became the chief theorist and propagandist for the Puritan cause. After the execution of Charles I and the interregnum, when Charles II returned to power in 1660, Milton was imprisoned and barely escaped execution. His blindness was

Chapter 2

advanced, however, and he was placed under house arrest with his daughters, where he was able to write poetry under scrutiny. After seven years he produced *Paradise Lost*, which can be read as in part a commentary upon and *apologia* for the failed Puritan rebellion in which he played such a prominent part.

The opening stanzas depict the fallen angels arriving in Hell after their defeat by the forces of Heaven; what should they do - give up in despair or find some way to continue the rebellion? Any Englishman of the time reading this opening would think immediately of the condition of the Puritan leaders in 1660, cast down to their surprise from the highest ranks to torment or death and unsure which path to take. Through his poem, Milton takes on the role of Lucifer (now 'Satan') illustrating a new path that may continue the rebellion. Milton then invokes another event from English history that should encourage them in this same direction.

The elevation of Jesus to the highest creature had traditionally been argued by invoking the Council of Nicaea, which taught that he had a human nature as well as a divine nature. Jesus's human nature was uniquely privileged in that it was suited to be joined to divinity, lifting it above every other human nature. In Milton's poem, Lucifer ignores this theological argument, choosing instead to distract his audience with a rebel-rousing, chest-beating, jingoistic screed, appealing to an 'all or nothing' ideology of freedom, hoping his audience will not notice that Milton is conflating Lucifer's audience of angels with his readership of 'free-born Englishmen'— evidently confident that the former will react identically to the latter.

This rhetorical distraction is announced in book 1, which strongly asserts that it is 'better to reign in Hell than serve in Heaven' (1.263). This 'all or nothing' ideology is expanded to full length in book 7:

> Thrones, Dominations, Princedoms, Virtues, Powers;
> If these magnific titles yet remain
> Not merely titular, since by decree
> Another now hath to himself engrossed
> All power, and us eclipsed under the name
> Of King anointed, for whom all this haste
> Of midnight-march, and hurried meeting here,

From Fusion to Divorce: The Reversal between Classical and Modern Overtures towards the Divine

> This only to consult how we may best,
> With what may be devised of honours new,
> Receive him coming to receive from us
> Knee-tribute yet unpaid, prostration vile!
> Too much to one! but double how endured,
> To one, and to his image now proclaimed?
> But what if better counsels might erect
> Our minds, and teach us to cast off this yoke?
> Will ye submit your necks, and choose to bend
> The supple knee? Ye will not, if I trust
> To know ye right, or if ye know yourselves
> Natives and sons of Heaven possessed before
> By none; and if not equal all, yet free,
> Equally free; for orders and degrees
> Jar not with liberty, but well consist.
> Who can in reason then, or right, assume
> Monarchy over such as live by right
> His equals, if in power and splendour less,
> In freedom equal? or can introduce
> Law and edict on us, who without law
> Err not? much less for this to be our Lord,
> And look for adoration, to the abuse
> Of those imperial titles, which assert
> Our being ordained to govern, not to serve.
> supremacy.

Lucifer's attempt to keep his fellow angels from accepting subordination to Jesus has been mapped onto and transposed into the historical resistance of the English barons on the fields of Runnymede in 1215 rejecting King John's attempt to extract higher taxes from them to fight his wars. The angels should follow their example and force their own *Magna Carta* upon the Almighty, defending their 'absolute' freedom and maintaining a wary suspicion against further incursions of illegitimate abuse of power.

Milton changes the 'key' in which God's announcement of the Incarnation is made to the angels: Jesus is God's Son, as is Lucifer. But God has unjustly elevated and appointed Jesus ruler over *all* creation, so that the angels now have *two* political superiors (God the Father and his 'image', Jesus) to whom they owe fealty and must bend the knee. This is presented as an intolerable affront to their status and injury to their liberty! The Incarnation is no longer a generous act of salvation on God's part to be celebrated with rejoicing, but a new set of manacles and chains the angels are asked to put on voluntarily without murmur. Milton/Lucifer claims that the Incarnation should be seen as a cause for grinding teeth, anger and rebellion.

This same opposition is present in more pointed or artistic fashion in the 'poetical and prophetic' works of William Blake, who wrote approximately fifty years later. Blake esteemed that he lived in a period when the human faculties, originally one, had become divided. He resurrected a form of the Platonic myth of the sexes as originally making together one 'giant' human being ('Albion') which had been split by the gods anxious at the strength of its powers and determined to keep it weak. Since the time of this separation the two sexes have been trying to get back together again, to regain their original strength.

Blake had been very independent as a child, to the point that his parents never required him to spend a single day in school; they foresaw that he would be rambunctious, incorrigible and disruptive. He was taught how to read at home, however, and henceforth became an autodidact. However, he was constitutionally averse to subordinating himself to any 'system'; his characteristic way of learning was to read a position, and then, in an independent second pulse-beat, use his imaginative and prophetic powers to improve or 'correct' the position he had taken in. For Blake this was the heartbeat of both human learning and history.

The goal, as always, was to re-achieve the original unity which had been lost. His views on empowerment did not extend as far as women, however. Although later he was in theoretical favor of woman's equality, he married an illiterate girl five years his junior whom he could instruct in his own views, and he regarded the first stage of the re-integration as involving woman's re-integration *within* man, not man's within woman, or man and woman together. Further, because Blake saw his era as arriving 'late in the game' after this splintering and alienation had proceeded for millennia, the separation of the original Albion into the 'Four Zoas' had already proceeded in an historical timeline that allowed Blake to produce his 'private mythology' in which he gave names to the parts that had become separate, and thus opposed and diseased. The primary hostility was between 'Urizen' who represented conventional religion with its repressive morality, as the high point of human culture and endeavor, associated with the God of the Old Testament, or 'God the Father.' Countering this constraint and repression, oppositional forces have grown up, represented by Luvah, Orc and Los, who stood for the power and legitimate rights of love, inspiration, imagination—and rebellion.

Unfortunately, because of the class-based monarchical oppression imposed by the inhibitory and enslaving dominance of Urizen, the only form that 'progress' could take now was this two-beat syncopation of first constraint and then revolt. There is no other way for us to work our way back towards our original unity and a redemptive integration. While such a rebellion does intend an ultimate integration with Urizen, because there are so many unities to be repaired and alienations to be overcome, this final culmination or *eschaton* recedes into the distance and almost disappears. In the short run the attitude of Christ-like progress away from the monarchical tradition of the self-interested control and intransigent privilege of Urizen must be unflinching opposition leading to wary caution, distrust and suspicion. This involves for the dawning Enlightenment mentality a turning away from the earlier goal of reconciliation and union through the now 'poisoned apple' of Christian Neo-Platonism, the 'Great Chain of Being' or the 'perennial philosophy'. The only prudent ethic is to abandon participation or 'fusion' with the deity as a personal or social ideal, in favor of a 'divorce' into 'independent operators', until revolutionary activity has produced a real change, such that it can then serve as evidence that re-integration is again desirable.

Chapter 3

Proportionate Love and Literature: The Revenge of the Bastard

The conviction that love should be proportionate to its object—that we get into trouble when we love an object either above or below its merits—was basic to Greek ethics and culture. Aristotle precipitated this conviction into a principle and analyzed moral virtue as the ability to discern a subjective mean between too much and too little in every area of conduct, together with the habitual exercise of hitting this mean. Excellence in this ability is a lifelong project, but as in all virtue, pleasure should kick in and reinforce our efforts as we begin to hit the target with regularity.

In a reverse mode, popular wisdom traced back social turmoil and political dysfunction to an absence of the proper love, esteem or sympathy that should characterize a relationship. René Girard has recently shown how competition leading to conflict is not an exceptional state of affairs in social organization, but rather is to be expected as the all-too-normal result of the natural dynamism of desire. In many traditional cultures, twins are left exposed to the elements to die. The 'official' reason is that the two improperly share one soul and thus cannot achieve normal fulfillment; the underlying reason is fear based on experience that the rivalry that normally characterizes siblings is exacerbated in the case of twins to break out in conflict, which not infrequently sweeps the family and wider social environment into a spiraling feud. Romulus and Remus, the mythological twins who founded Rome, were thrown into the Tiber at birth, but a she-wolf rescued and suckled them; after they matured, Romulus killed Remus in a dispute over where Rome should be located.

The historical books of the Old Testament are replete with perverted relationships which have devastating consequences for the family and wider community. Because polygamy is the norm, illegitimacy is not an issue, but marginality and a sense of injured or unrecognized merit certainly are. Cain kills Abel because his sacrifice is not deemed as worthy as his brother's; the concubine Hagar becomes proud of her pregnancy, taunts the barren wife Sarai who so abuses her that she runs away. Joseph is the spoiled younger son whom his older brothers resent. Saul becomes darkly embittered at David's military success and consequent greater popularity. David loves Absolom, perhaps because Absolom is the man he should have been, but is not; Absolom detests David, rebuffs and rebels against him, perhaps for the same reason.

While Christianity did not favor viewing the traditional family as a conflictual state, by imposing monogamy, it opened the door to the artistic depiction of illegitimacy as a dangerous practice primarily because of the failed affection it insinuated and poisoned relationships it propagated. The illegitimate son legitimately *dis*-affects his father, who has forgotten him and typically fails to acknowledge him. Yet because a son's identity derives initially from the father, the link cannot be broken. The illegitimate son grieves for his lost relationship, sometimes giving in to recrimination and rancor against the person who has sired him and whom he has a right to love; at other times he will rebel or in some fashion seek revenge for the natural relationship to which he feels entitled but of which he has been cheated. This perverse inversion of proportionate love can result in an offspring who feels deprived, exacting revenge some years later. It is a hurt that is not assuaged and does not go away. The American abolitionist Frederick Douglass writes in his autobiography of his pain at seeing the man he took to be his father, the master of the plantation on which his mother worked as a slave, show no remorse for what he had done nor take any responsibility for the consequences.

Artists in the Christian West were not slow to tap the device of the smoldering bastard—or heir bypassed because he was born under the *bar sinistre* or wrong side of the bed—to explain ongoing complaint or a surprising eruption of violence after years of quiet and apparently torpid resignation. Shakespeare's plays—like aristocratic Renaissance society itself—are full of lesser sons and illegitimate heirs condemned to well-heeled social parasitism and political irrelevance because of the 'sin of the father'. Typically they bide their time, waiting for a chance to lead a rebellion and seize by force the post they claim should be theirs by right. Dramatically, however, the pathos of impotence and unmerited injury are better perceived in those figures who have no chance of reversing the cruel destiny a self-indulgent and now absent paternity has dealt them. The latter show their condition as one of shame and teeth-grinding frustration.

In Shakespeare's *The Tempest*, illegitimacy is compounded with miscegenation to produce our first portrait of a creature confused in his physical appearance, his social status and his deeper psychological condition. Prospero is the ruler of a mysterious island that seems a cross between Robinson Crusoe's cannibal habitat and the recently discovered Bermuda. He has a servant Caliban, whom he refers to as a brutal savage, and who is treated as a figure of fun and contempt by all the characters. He is described as a 'mooncalf', a 'freckled whelp', and is thought of as a wild man, a beast man or a fish-man. Everyone is confused about who he is—including himself. Although he was the only human inhabitant of the island, he is not native; according to Prospero he is the son of the witch Sycorax by a devil. Sycorax was banished from Australia, abandoned on the strange isle pregnant with Caliban and died before Prospero's arrival. Caliban is clearly in psychological pain and not at home with himself; two ways he seeks relief are by forcing acceptance from the more self-assured later arrivals, Prospero and his family, and overcoming his loneliness by producing others like himself. Prospero justifies his harsh treatment of Caliban by saying that after initially befriending him, Caliban tried to rape his daughter Miranda. Caliban gleefully confirms this, saying that if he hadn't been stopped, he would have peopled the island with a race of Calibans. He is thus essentially lonely—and never more so than when surrounded by these different people from across the sea. Unable to win acceptance, his mind swings to the opposite strategy. Referring to his mother's god as Setebos, he belies his surface good humor and shows his deeper resentment of Prospero. Stephano, one of the shipwrecked servants, has given Caliban some wine; Caliban takes Stephano as his god and new master. He urges Stephano to kill Prospero and become lord of the island. He dreams of dispelling his sense of discomfort and marginality; one day his time may come:

Be not afeared; the isle is full of noises,
Sounds and sweet airs, that give delight and hurt not.
Sometimes a thousand twanging instruments
Will hum about mine ears, and sometimes voices
That, if I then had waked after long sleep,
Will make me sleep again; and then, in dreaming,
The clouds methought would open and show riches
Ready to drop upon me; that, when I waked,
I cried to dream again.   Act 3, scene 2

In Fyodor Dostoevsky's *The Brothers Karamozov*, Smerdyakov is the illegitimate fourth son of Fyodor Pavlovich Karamozov, a sponger and buffoon who has taken no interest in any of his sons (from two marriages). As a result, they were raised apart from each other and from the father. Smerdyakov kills Fyodor but commits suicide before he can be detected, and Dimitri, the eldest son, is put on trial. Dimitri is a sensualist like his father, and would have a motive for the crime in the money he needs for his life of debauchery and gambling. Ivan is the second son, the first by Fyodor's second marriage. He is a sensitive rationalist appalled at the suffering in the world and the unrepentant evil in most people, like his father and brother. His sensitivity leads him to become sullen and withdrawn from everyone around him. His hatred for his father is not openly expressed, but indirectly contributes to his daringly 'modern' and shocking atheism.

Smerdyakov was born of 'Stinking Lizaveta', a mute woman of the streets from whom his name comes —'Son of the reeking one'. He serves as a lackey and cook for his father, but is not acknowledged as one of the family. He is morose and sullen, and like Dostoevsky himself, an epileptic. As a child he would hang stray cats and later bury them. Smerdyakov is aloof with most people but admires Ivan, whose atheistic philosophy affords him an indirect outlet for his own negative feelings. It is Ivan who tells him that if God does not exist, then 'everything is permitted'. Whereas Ivan is a cold theorist, however, Smerdyakov is a man of action.

Late in the novel Smerdyakov confesses to Ivan that he and not Dimitri is the murderer, yet he claims to have acted with Ivan's blessing. It seems to be Ivan's recognition of the truth in this statement, through both his hatred of the father and the tacit authorization his philosophy supplied, that drives him to insanity. Smerdyakov is not as stupid as he looks, however, nor gullible; he is easily capable of exploiting Ivan's sensitivity to manipulate him into sharing his guilt. Dimitri's defense attorney points out that he found Smerdyakov 'falsely naïve', that he can divine people's weaknesses, especially evil intentions; he then tells them what they want to hear to insinuate his own ideas within them. He is more of a Svengali than a victim.

Dostoevsky clearly believes the father drove his sons to this deed, and that in some sense it was a communal act. Only Alyosha escapes the contaminating poison through his religious vocation. The others are sinned against, but carry on in various ways the evil they have inherited, harming all who come close, including one another. Smerdyakov, his revenge sated, does not hesitate to take his own life.

In a brief third example, the 2007 Zemeckis film version of *Beowulf* unifies the story over the original version in a way that shows the human mind moving naturally in this direction. In the original, Grendel and his mother are said to be evil simply because they are 'children of Cain'; the film, however, uncovers a deeper link. The principle of proportionate love injects a nerve to the plot, unifies the two halves, and lifts the saga above heroic exploits by infusing at its core a piece of folk wisdom that gives the audience something to mull over.

King Hrothgar has an affair with a water demon years before the story begins; the result is the monster Grendel, who as the story opens is harassing his father's mead hall from pain and rage at his carousing parent who has, in effect, forgotten and disowned him. A young warrior from Geatsland, Beowulf, comes to slay the monster to earn glory. He kills Grendel and tracks his mother to her lair; instead of killing her, however, he too is seduced, which produces a second monster that years later will become Beowulf's own nemesis. The mother, apparently also angry at her years of neglect, returns the golden drinking horn that signified their peace bargain. When Beowulf tries to give it back, she refuses to take it, releasing instead the dragon they have together spawned. Beowulf is barely able to destroy it before it exacts revenge by killing both his wife and his mistress; the battle is too much for him in his advanced years, however. He dies, restoring the order to his family and his kingdom he had slowly built up, which his sexual dalliance, like that of Hrothgar before him, had needlessly imperiled. The unspoken moral is, rather than have to perform such a Herculean labor and perhaps suffer a final tragedy, wouldn't it be better from the start to avoid such a provocation? If 'hell hath no fury like a woman scorned', the simmering resentment of a bastard child runs a close second.

Chapter 4

Apocalypto, The Explosion/Debunking of the 'Noble Savage', and with it of Enlightenment Ethics

Mel Gibson's movie *APOCALYPTO* calls into question the 'noble savage' by depicting indigenous Mayans engaging in human sacrifice, and also questions the deeper belief among 'post-Christian' Europeans in a 'universal natural ethic' which is superior to Christianity and that all people everywhere observe.

Mel Gibson's 2006 film *APOCALYPTO* was unusual in several respects. First of all, it was filmed entirely with indigenous actors speaking a Mayan dialect (with subtitles). As a 'western', it was strange in that its action took place before the arrival of Europeans, so the 'action' involved no interaction between those two groups. In fact, the film concludes with the first view of a Spanish ship to arrive in Central America, with the indigenous characters, who have been through a shattering experience (and probably thought that their unusual or difficult experiences were over), staring in stunned disbelief at this first-ever event in their culture. What significance does Mel Gibson mean us to attach to this?

The film begins with an extensive section depicting the indigenous warm and affectionate family life; there are events common to all families, and much humor. It is easy for the viewer to overcome all sense of alienation and conclude, 'You see, they are just like we are.' But then a hunting party emerges from the jungle and chases down the inhabitants of this village. It turns out that they are from a different, and stronger branch of the Maya, and are seeking victims to offer to their high gods as human sacrifices.

This is far from an unusual event in this culture; in fact, it is quite normal or typical for branches of the Maya to wage war to acquire captives and then transport them to their high altars built with impressive stone and rich carvings, to be kept as privileged prisoners until the day when they will be taken up *en masse* to have their hearts cut out and heads bloodied until their lifeless bodies are thrown down the steep steps to be collected in a pile at the bottom. Although painful to witness, it is not the purpose of the film to shock us by their brutality; in fact, it is the intent of the film to make us realize how usual and regular this is within their culture. Human sacrifice is the way to give highest praise and worship to their gods. It is the way to offer the most valuable thing we possess to the highest beings in the universe, to obtain their good will and continued support for our crops and related economic-political-military activities. Although subordinate clans are not necessarily happy at having to supply these victims, they must grudgingly admit this behavior is what you would expect from the highest culture.

In fact, what the audience comes to notice is that, after you have gotten over your squeamishness at this brutal treatment, this is a picture with no 'heroes'. That is, the clans on the bottom of the social pyramid, who currently supply victims for the sacrifices, would do exactly the same thing if suddenly they came to occupy the top spot, or become the leading clan. The power of the film comes from the fact that the viewer is thrown off center, thoroughly disoriented and confused. Their social world has been ripped from them. Without knowing who to support or who to oppose, the viewer doesn't know what the director expects him to experience, or what to do with their emotion. One isn't sure what kind of emotional release one should be having—if any.

One effect of this experience is that it forces you to take seriously the indigenous world view—and to compare it with one's own. On the natural level it makes perfect sense. Blood is the most valuable human commodity. Mayan nobles used to deliberately puncture their skin with thorns, needles or sting ray spines as a means to achieve communion, harmony and peace with their gods. Such an experience achieves the highest level of intimacy and communion with the divine open to man. Such language is not foreign to the Christian tradition: in holy communion, Christ invites us to consume his 'body and blood', as he shared bread and wine with his disciples during the Last Supper. Christians pursue a symbolic union; the Mayans, without this symbolic option, sought a literal union. It is in making 'the old strange' and 'the new acceptable' that the film assaults our senses and minds by calling the deepest assumptions of our world into question.

Once before in the contemporary period an artist achieved this effect, but its intent was more superficial and designed simply to shock. In 1948 Shirley Jackson published a short story in *The New Yorker* entitled *The Lottery*. It began as the simple story of a rural community assembling at a center for its annual festival. Everything is familiar and traditional; it is a time for seeing old friends and celebrating another year—until the final sentence, which informs us that the members conclude by picking up rocks and stoning an unfortunate young woman who has been chosen as this year's victim for the sacrifice. The members' lack of emotion or comment is meant to contrast with unspoken hysterics among the readers. The story was meant to shock the conventional pieties of post-World War II America, which was hoping to leave violence behind and get back to a 'civilized' way of life. It had no deeper ambition; the same cannot be said of Gibson's film.

The image of the 'noble savage' was part of an ideological assault by the Enlightenment on the very notion of a 'Christian State' as the ideal of Western Civilization since Constantine accepted Christianity as the official religion for his Empire in the fourth century. The Enlightenment wanted to separate the West from its thousand-year tradition of official Christian allegiance, in preference for and to expose the merely 'natural' foundations for a state that were still present from its 'pagan' past. The Enlightenment program was to scrape off the Christian patina from western intellectual development, leaving behind the previous pagan or 'natural' intellectual foundation that had laid undisturbed and dormant below it down the centuries, so that it was now fit to be re-discovered and re-installed as the basis for a purely 'natural' system of ethics and politics (that would also be acceptable to non-Christians and atheists in the West). Rousseau is the apostle and evangelist of this new gospel; he concomitantly raised the hope of discovering in the 'heathen' colonies this 'natural virtue' incarnate in an unconverted 'noble savage' who would lead 'European man' back to his proper development. Thus the American Indian was studied carefully for more than simply his curious folkways; he became a crucial piece in the ideological program to fortify the Enlightenment attack on the 'artificial' and 'unnatural' European ways that had grown up and as the indication of a more accurate, adequate and indeed excellent way of life. A tremendous ideological weight thus fell on such unprepossessing and supposedly 'unambitious' sociological investigations. Europe waited with mounting anticipation to see whether they would lead us back to our ancient greatness, or disappoint us by producing merely a degenerate mongrel like Caliban in Shakespeare's *The Tempest*, set in recently-discovered Bermuda.

So what is Mel Gibson's verdict? What does he mean to say by having the first sailing ship of the Spanish Empire appear in the lagoon in the last scene of his film? Generally we would have to say it represents a 'No' to the question of whether there is such a thing as a 'noble savage' (a judgment made in the violent first part of the film) but also as to whether there is such a thing as a beneficent 'Enlightenment ethic' (represented by the newly arriving Spanish in the second half). The Europeans will only superficially overthrow the cruel tyranny and exploitation of native peoples in the New World by virtue of their Christian faith; it is more accurate to say they will invade, defeat and exploit their advantage in war through disease, steel and gun powder to achieve an even more vicious and cruel victory and stranglehold over the native inhabitants, leading to their enslavement as human chattel as an offering to the feverish search for gold, silver and other forms of wealth that could be transferred back to Europe. The newly-arriving Spanish are no exception to the already-established pattern of mutual enslavement and exploitation among the diverse American tribes, but will only install a more cruel and successful form of exploitation and eventual annihilation of the native stock in exchange for legal tender, mined specie and other forms of wealth.

As Gibson was born in America and raised in Australia (both 'Enlightenment' counties by their founding documents and early history), there is a fine distinction and irony between the way this dire verdict and message is delivered in the 'old world' of Europe (where the Enlightenment debate took place) and the 'new world' of the Americas and the colonies generally where its practical consequences will dictate the structure of a new society. A pessimistic 'No' to the Enlightenment debate as to whether there is such a thing as 'Enlightenment ethics' would serve as a social distraction and amusement, an artistic bauble, an intellectual pastime in the traditional cities, classrooms and estates of the European masters; in the novel and unprecedented political experiments of post-revolutionary new world 'democracies', it takes on an immediate practical relevance and terrifying vital impulse. Those Europeans who were transported or chose to emigrate to the 'new' Enlightenment territories were potentially both masters *and* slaves, the exploiters *and* the exploited, under these new regimes and circumstances. They had a practical interest in the outcome of the abstract debate which their continental ancestors and contemporaries did not have. In a sense, they had to extract a 'Yes' vote to the theoretical question because without this the viability of their political system and practical experiment would lose its foundation, and vanish.

Gibson stays mum. Whether he has personal views or not, the film leaves us hanging. There simply *is* no conclusion. It terminates on the level of entertainment with the natives dumbstruck and staring in awe at the newly-arrived transport marvels from another world. There is not yet any disease, steel weapons or gun powder: all that lies in the future, down to colonial Belgium in the Congo where King Leopold authorizes amputating the limbs of recalcitrant natives who did not work fast enough - while Joseph Conrad takes notes on shipboard on this 'heart of darkness'—helping us, perhaps, towards an answer to the question.

Chapter 5

The Devil Made Me Do It: How the West Disguised its Diabolical Switch of Messiah

I propose an 'intellectual genealogy' of the widespread contemporary lifestyle called 'expressive individualism', tracing it back first to the cult of the artist as genius, which flourished during the 19th century, which has been democratized and universalized in our time. I then trace it one step further back, somewhat surprisingly, to the altered depiction of Lucifer John Milton gives in his poem *Paradise Lost*. Milton's Lucifer rejects not only Jesus as the highest creature, he rejects the Father as father; he announces 'I know none before me; I am self-begot.' In other words, he has fathered himself. This represents a more radical rebellion and deeper alienation than in the traditional story. The artist as genius also says 'I know none before me; I am self-begot.' I argue that the artist as genius is a literary descendant, specifically a secularization, of Milton's revised angelology, to the extent that when we embrace the ethic of 'expressive individualism', we are implicitly committed to Milton's Lucifer as the archetype for human fulfillment—which I suggest is a toxic model.

In book X of the *Republic*, Plato famously contrasts the influence of the poets with the philosophers. Specifically, the poets always have more influence than the philosophers; that's what makes poetry so dangerous. Philosophy makes demands upon us, sometimes requires changes and can be difficult; the audience for it is small. On the other hand, as Shelley famously proclaimed, poets are the 'unacknowledged legislators of the world.' History bears out this preponderant influence of poetry over both science and philosophy. David Hume complained that his early work, *A Treatise on Human Nature,* 'fell stillborn from the press.' Nobody bought it or indeed took any notice of it, despite its importance. Indeed, it was Emanuel Kant who made David Hume famous as a philosopher, specifically by being provoked by Hume's philosophy to create his own; during his lifetime, Hume was more famous for his historical works. It is because of this disproportionate influence that Plato would have poetry banned from his ideal republic. In book ten, as said, he imagines accompanying the poets to the frontiers of his ideal state and praising them even as he insists they have to go. The poets are *too* powerful. Their creations enchant us and easily sweep us unawares into error and illusion. Odysseus strapped himself to the mast of his vessel so that he could listen to the sirens' song without being lured to his death, but in a polity the poets can have no such place, for there is no analogue to the mast protecting us against the spells they weave.

My thesis is that our society is no different, and that a single poet has had a disproportionate influence over the whole of the modern period; further, this influence is the more powerful in that it has gone largely unrecognized. That poet is not Shakespeare, nor is it Dante. It is not Virgil, the poet of the Roman Empire, nor Homer the bard of the Greeks. That poet is John Milton, the author of *Paradise Lost*, and the influence comes through the tractor beam drawing us towards his most dramatic creation, Lucifer, the prince of the archangels, or 'Satan' as he is called in the poem after his fall from heaven. We sometimes think that philosophy gives the nod to art, but in fact the relation is usually the other way around. In ancient Greece relatively few people read Plato or Aristotle, but Homer was universally venerated. Similarly, in the Middle Ages Augustine and Thomas Aquinas were accessible to fewer than knew Virgil, Boccaccio or Chaucer. The modern period is less an age of Descartes, Locke and Kant than an age of Milton, of whose audacity the others could view as specifications; similarly, the contemporary period has been less intrigued by Heidegger and Wittgenstein than captivated by Pirandello, Camus and Ingmar Bergman.

There have been indications for some time that Milton's Lucifer is at the origin of the modern cult of the artist as 'genius'. The cultural prestige of *Paradise Lost* as 'the Protestant Epic', the response to Dante's *Divine Comedy* written three centuries earlier, has discouraged attention from the ways Milton changes the received story, and as a consequence from the ways both the project and motivation of the modern artist differ from the mimetic enterprise of pre-modern art. It was the British Romantic poets—Lord Byron, Wordsworth, Keats, Shelley and Coleridge—who more than a century after Milton's death, reached back over the neo-classical poets John Dryden and Alexander Pope, who were poets of the Stuart restoration, to John Milton, and specifically to his overpowering creation, Lucifer, to fashion the archetype of human perfection for the modern period, the artist as 'genius'. The reason these poets were drawn to Milton was that his poetry contained what the neo-classical poets lacked—the elements of awe, fascination and danger, which would be woven together to produce the Romantic 'sublime'. These poets abandoned Milton's Christian apology and extracted the element of enhanced rebellion and unprecedented defiance in Milton's novel portrait, transferring this trait from the angelic to the human realm, to fashion the archetype of the artist as 'genius'. With the cultural decline of the saint and even the scientist as influential alternatives to this powerful icon, the artist as genius continues almost by default to chart the parameters for human achievement and perfection in the modern age; under different names and in various guises, he continues to function as our model and pattern for human fulfillment. My thesis is that the artist as genius should be understood as genetically a secularization of Milton's revised angelology; our culture for the past four hundred years is for this reason most accurately described as Luciferian.

First a bit of background. I got into this study by looking into 'celebrity culture'. Celebrities play a major role in our society. The first observation was that they depend upon the media; in fact, they need one another. Celebrities sell media, and media promote celebrities; it is a symbiotic relationship. This is true for all the more recent media—radio, movies, television, you-tube, facebook, etc.—but also for the first medium—the book. The first European 'best seller' was Goethe's novel *The Sufferings of Young Werther—Die Leiden des Jungen Werther* (1774). Werther was a sort of proto-Romantic figure, like his *Wilhelm Meister*. So popular was young Werther that young men began to dress like him. He is described in the novel as favoring yellow waistcoats, and this seems to have created a run on yellow waistcoats in men's fashion. This led to a second insight. We say that 'Art imitates Nature'. Well, it is equally true that 'Nature imitates Art', that is, that human nature is prone to model itself on the heroes or heroines it finds in art. We need archetypes to serve as ideals for our behavior and ambitions. In this regard, Goethe's novel had an unfortunate effect. The story is a sad one, for at its conclusion young Werther takes his own life. Well, it is reported that a few young men wanted to model themselves on Werther so desperately that they committed suicide—with a copy of the novel in their back pockets! This is probably an exaggeration, but so powerful could be the attraction of a hero or ideal—even one who is only fictional.

This led me to examine the role of archetypes in a culture—a Jungian analysis—and I came to the conclusion that the nineteenth century was drawn in two opposite directions, or was pursuing two different archetypes—the scientist and the artist as genius. These two clashed, they produced a shirring effect upon the mind; they rendered the culture bi-polar or schizophrenic. More deeply, there was a division between two opposed world views: on the one hand the prospect of a completely mechanized or determined universe, and on the other the Romantic celebration, indeed the glorification and deification of the artistic genius as not only free, but as an original and creative spirit. This opposition brought about a crisis of values in the 19th century. Let us look at this more closely.

First science. The search for law-like behaviour had made enormous strides during the Enlightenment through the work of Descartes, Galileo, Newton, Huygens, Lavoisier, Robert Boyle and Joseph Priestly in creating a mechanistic science of the inorganic world. During the nineteenth century there was a push to extend the reach of law-like behavior from the inorganic to the organic realm, and even into the human sphere. Darwin achieved success with his theory of evolution, and there were attempts to discover law-like behavior in the fields we know today as psychology, sociology, economics and even history (Karl Marx thought there were laws to history). The more adventuresome spirits, like the American Ralph Waldo Emerson in his 1836 essay *Nature*, urged us not to be afraid or hold back from this intoxicating, sublime vision, not to continue making an *exception* of ourselves, but to have the courage to embrace this apparent dissolution of the self, involved in the full acceptance of universally deterministic science that the 'atheist' Spinoza had misread, not seeing the deeper triumph that awaits us on its far side:

The Devil Made Me Do It: How the West Disguised its Diabolical Switch of Messiah

'Standing on the bare ground, my head bathed by the blithe air, and uplifted into infinite space,—all mean egotism vanishes. I become a transparent eyeball; I am nothing; I see all; the currents of Universal Being circulate through me; I am part or particle of God.'

The poet Shelley posited the same basis for the rapturous Romantic Sublime:

I am the eye with which the Universe
Beholds itself, and knows it is divine . . .

Scientific determinism was therefore not necessarily opposed to Romanticism; indeed, the final 'determination from within' may have been the goal of history. Such determinism rather supports and reinforces the latter by encouraging us to merge ourselves back into the universe and become the one point where the resulting complex advances to clear ideas and higher self-knowledge—since the 'self' in this sense is the only thing there is to be known.

Not only was scientific theory making great strides, but practical science, or engineering, was making impressive breakthroughs as well. There were 'World Expositions'— in London in 1851, which built the 'Crystal Palace', the largest covered space in the world up to that point, made of state-of-the-art materials such as steel and glass, which put on display inventions and new devices that would make our lives more efficient and comfortable. Another exposition was held in Paris in 1880 where the engineer Eiffel built his famous tower, which was so impressive it was left afterwards to grace the Parisian skyline.

So confident was this expansionist movement that it was thought that science was nearly over; the edifice of mechanistic science almost complete. There were laws that we hadn't discovered yet, but so organized and coordinated was research at that moment that it would be only decades before we would have completed the job. The end is within sight. It is difficult for us today to capture the sense of triumph and smug self-confidence, in this age of steamships and railways, that the leaders of government, industry and commerce had in the pending complete subjugation of nature—which means our entire phenomenal world—to mechanistic laws. This exhilarating prospect had its proponents and popularizers, taming and rendering palatable the still-dreaded spectre of Spinoza, in whose vision all human action would freeze into an icy necessitarian grip. In England, Herbert Spencer, Thomas Huxley and H. G. Wells celebrated humanity's oneness with the natural world and pursued a program of 'unified science' (with Thomas Kuhn's later work on 'paradigm shifts', enthusiasm for this earlier vision faded.) In the German world, Rudolf Carnap, Moritz Schlick, Max Stirner and Friedrich Nietzsche turned against the 'sentimentality' of neo-Kantianism's making a 'protected exception' of loyalty to freedom. In France, August Compte constructed his Positivistic philosophy while Jules Vern churned out futuristic adventure novels. All looked forward enthusiastically and rapturously to the imminent completion and triumph of the scientific enterprise. Politically speaking, it could be said that nationalism and science had replaced the Holy Roman Empire and Christianity as our primary allegiances and instruments to bring history to its culmination; quite simply, they had done the job better than the earlier candidates. Not only did science give us a more precise and complete vision of the universe, but with its greater power and final completion we could, somewhat paradoxically, announce there would be no more wars! It surprises and embarrasses us today to notice how naïve national leaders were that the *entente cordiale* that prevailed after the breakup of Napoleon's empire would succeed—perhaps with the help of these new 'laws' from the social sciences—to isolate any eruption of violence in the resulting population and prevent these from spreading and escalating into a larger conflagration. Of course, they were aware that this same science had produced an arsenal of weapons considerably more powerful than had ever been produced before—dynamite, the machine gun, nerve gas, etc.—but they were sure these could be controlled and probably never be used. Why, it would be madness! Even if you won such a war, your losses would be so great as to make the conflict prohibitively expensive in human terms. So then, we *have* done the job! We have reached the 'end of history'—Kant's dream of 'perpetual peace' - even before Fukujama's recent book announced it. We have reached the *eschaton*, the final stage of human history—a secular *eschaton* of course, but an *eschaton* nonetheless. And we have done so by ourselves!

The Devil Made Me Do It: How the West Disguised its Diabolical Switch of Messiah

Of course, time itself will not stop, and science will continue to make incremental advances in the future, but *grosso modo* we may announce that we have reached the final stage which modern culture has long sought. We have a right to feel relieved and proud of our accomplishment, to pat ourselves on the back for having had the courage and perseverance to question received ideas, to gratefully accept the reward for which we have long labored, which we have well and truly merited.

Of course, there is a price to pay. There are always casualties that come with any serious change in our world view. One victim is God. Since the rise of Deism, the only God we could salvage has been a 'god of the gaps', but unfortunately the 'gaps' have grown smaller over time; so that now there is almost no job left for God to help us out with. Science has stepped in and is doing most of the heavy lifting we used to need God to perform. When the mathematician Laplace presented his model of the cosmos to Napoleon, Napoleon complained, 'But where is God in your universe?', Laplace responded: '*Sire, je n'ai pas besoin de cette hypothese.*' Candidly, there was a cultural nostalgia, a temporary sense of loss and sadness in even the hardest spirits. In 1867, Matthew Arnold published *Dover Beach*—still the most anthologized poem in the English language. He used the outgoing tide as an image for religious faith. During the Middle Ages the sea of Christianity had rushed in, spreading over all of Europe. Now that tide had turned and was flowing out—you can hear the waves slapping on the bare rocks—never to return.

There were other, this-worldly casualties as well—specifically freedom and value. It was again the mathematician Laplace who hypothesized that if there were an omniscient demon who knew the laws of nature as well as the location and velocity of every particle in the universe, he could predict forwards and backwards to all eternity the location and movement of those same particles. Not only was there no gap for God, there was no gap for freedom. But if we embrace the prospect of an all-embracing determinism, this has devastating consequences for our lives. Can I really begin something new, or make any real difference in the universe? I become more languid or less ambitious, feeling myself sapped of initiative and industry. Everything seems fixed ahead of time - so why make any effort? I can neither speed things up nor slow them down. *Que será, será*. I am headed for a species of paralysis. But can an indolent life really be satisfying - or 'happy'? Both John Stuart Mill and William James tried to reconcile the scientific worldview with a convincing sense of human freedom, and both suffered a psychological breakdown.

Suppose we protest, saying 'Look, I *am* free. I can either raise my hand or lower it. Nothing forces me one way or the other—nothing compels me. What is actual must be possible; if I can *commit* a free act, freedom must be real. It is your theory, rather than reality, that falls short.' Our opponent might respond: 'Listen, what you call an *experience* of freedom might just be your *ignorance* of laws that even now are secretly controlling and determining your behavior. The fact that you do not experience these laws does not prove they do not exist. If I knew more about you—who your parents were, who your grandparents were, what your DNA is, what culture you belong to, what you ate for breakfast, etc.—perhaps I could predict that on this day, at this time you would raise your hand. Maybe in twenty or thirty years we will have uncovered the psychological, sociological or economic laws that explain your behavior. This has happened in the past; why could it not happen again in the future?'

More seriously, with the loss of freedom goes the loss of value. If everything is determined, nothing is higher or lower than anything else; they are all connected points in a matrix, a solid brick. If we are all linked by laws, we are just parts of one big thing. In fact, there really is only one 'thing'—the universe as a whole. We can't pretend that we can 'cherry-pick' the parts we like, and somehow get rid of the others. We cannot separate the two; it's a block universe. Pick any one piece, and you're stuck with the whole thing. Otherwise expressed, the principle of individuation does not cut very deep. You and I look as if we were separate from one another—as if we were autonomous and free—but if we are connected by myriad laws like puppets on strings, then this appearance is an illusion. We are bound tightly together by invisible threads. The universe is a 'package deal'; it's all or nothing, take it or leave it.

So whatever mechanistic science might bring us by way of material benefit, comfort or security, we have the disturbing feeling that something important has been lost—that something essential has been removed from the table. The mathematician and philosopher Blaise Pascal expressed this apprehension with his lament: '*Le silence éternal de ces espaces infinis m'effraie*'. Not only is God now a question mark, but all values are up for grabs. Specifically, if freedom is the basis of whatever dignity humans enjoy over the rest of nature, and if there *is* no freedom, we may treat humans the same way we treat everything else. There is no higher status. This is disquieting; we can perhaps do without God, but can we really live without values?

In this crisis the Romantic notion of the artist as genius initially came to the rescue by providing a response to this loss. Whereas ordinary people may be repetitive and mechanical in their behavior—coerced by the invisible laws of nature—the genius is identified as original and creative. He is constantly generating value through the masterpieces he is churning out through his art. (All geniuses were initially imagined as male; in many countries women didn't even get the vote until the twentieth century.) It started in late Eighteenth-century England, with Edward Young's *Conjectures on Original Composition* (1759). Addison and Steel, the editors of the proto-newspapers *The Tatler* and *The Spectator,* started using 'genius' in this expanded sense, and Dr. Johnson, the compiler of the original dictionary, followed suit. This 'artist-as-genius' emerged as an ideological construct for the rescue and 'salvation' of mankind from the death grip of mechanistic determinism.

Geniuses were thought of as thick on the ground in 19th-century Europe, especially in Paris—poets, novelists, sculptors, painters, composers, musicians, dancers and so on.[1] Actuality implies possibility; if there *are* geniuses, as there manifestly seemed to be, then they must be possible. This means we can relax, exhale and stop worrying; we won't have to do without value. The genius will offer us what God or the world have ceased to supply, he will take up the slack and make up for the loss! During the 19th century artistic geniuses were considered an elite—almost a distinct species separate from ordinary people. Nevertheless, their presence assured us that we could accept the philosophical loss of God and freedom without having to radically rearrange our worldview or seriously alter our lifestyle. We would still have value; the artist-as-genius has picked up the baton that God appears to have dropped. We can keep going to the opera, to the ballet, to the art gallery and the theater—but less often to church—because this world of values remains intact. It is in good hands, alive and well. So again—we can exhale, relax, experience relief and release from our cultural anxieties—nothing important has been lost. An alien species from a distant planet has fortunately arrived to replace the absent deity. This solution left us not only with a theory, but also with a *cult*. We *worship* the artist as genius. Why? Because he is the sole source of value in an otherwise valueless world. He has what we need, and he is the only place we can get it—so we pay him top dollar.

What exactly *is* the genius? Can we specify him more precisely? From ancient times a celebrated artist has always received honor, but during the Romantic period, with metaphysics disqualified by Kant from constituting our highest activity or even contributing to knowledge, art has been drafted to fill the void; the status of the artist began to rise correspondingly. Kant tried to integrate the genius into the wider Enlightenment worldview, specifically, to relate him to the emerging deterministic view of science. All humans, as members of the phenomenal world, are 'horizontally' determined by the laws of nature. If you drop me out a window, I will fall with the same velocity as a pencil or stone. But humans have a foot in the 'noumenal' realm as well, to the extent that they hear the voice of conscience or are subject to the moral law, which Kant called 'the categorical imperative'. Humans are distinctive in experiencing moral conflict, and are free to obey or disobey the moral law; what they are not free to do is to ignore or escape it. For Kant, this constitutes access to a realm distinct from and higher than the world of material objects, for it is a realm where freedom is real. The artist as genius transcends the mechanical world to an even greater extent by being able to act with *originality* or *creativity*. He or she may become 'internally' determined. According to Kant, such free causality or creativity need involve no violation of the laws of nature. The 'Idealist' and 'Pessimistic' followers of Kant—Hegel and Schopenhauer—agreed in subscribing to and celebrating the artistic 'genius' as distinct, and indeed engaging in this highest form of human activity. Apart from moral experience, the rest of humankind is confined to the 'phenomenal' order; the genius, however, puts us in contact with the 'noumenal' world, the realm of freedom and creativity, to which we can be lifted up as we attend through the experience of art. There is thus a vestigial religious sensibility or dimension attributed to art, in that we are 'lifted up' or 'saved' - but now from mechanistic determinism rather than from sin or evil. 'Noumenal' and 'phenomenal' thereby become loose cultural analogues or philosophical replacements for the basic distinction on which western culture had been based. The genius becomes our 'saviour', our redeemer, who descends to rescue and lift us up to a higher realm. The genius replaces the saint of the Middle Ages, and the 'scientist' of the Enlightenment, as the acme of human self-actualization and pinnacle of human achievement, the archetype who makes possible an unsuspected alternative—an improbably fortunate form of human redemption, a last outpost of human worth.

Robert Bellah coined the term 'expressive individualism' in his book *Habits of the Heart* (1985); the term was then taken up and expanded by Charles Taylor in Chapter 13 of *A Secular Age* (2007). Taylor follows Lionel Trilling in charting the romantic revolt against neo-classical constraints, throwing off subservience to external norms and formal rules, privileging first 'sincerity', meaning an external expression that mirrors and matches one's interior feelings, and then the more demanding Existential call for 'authenticity'. In *A Secular Age,* Taylor explores in detail the lifestyle of 'expressive individualism' as this descends from the Romantic movement, and has invaded the contemporary consumer culture. He addresses such issues as the sexual revolution, the call to openness and a toleration of divergent lifestyles, the concentration on self-fulfillment, the smorgasbord, pick-and-choose approach to religion, fashion, politics, education, marriage and leisure time activities, that illustrate and fill out how this lifestyle has become the default ethos of our time.

What exactly is 'expressive individualism'? It's the set of priorities that comes to us through the media, through television, movies, advertising, but also now through the newer technologies of videos, the internet, Facebook, blogging, texting, twitter, etc. It was noticed first among the celebrities who serve as models for many of our youth. People become celebrities in various ways—forming rock bands, acting in TV commercials or soap-operas, becoming champions in sports, fashion models, stand-up comedians, news announcers or weather girls. The goal is to achieve name and face recognition. Once this is attained, they may branch out into other media possibilities to take full advantage of their 'bankable' status, go on world tours or start TV talk shows and become social pundits. The first obligation of course is to stay in the public eye, which is necessary for any entertainer. There is nothing wrong with this, but because of the need to retain public attention in an increasingly competitive field, there is inevitably pressure to be novel, original or different. This can lead to bizarre outfits, roles and performances.

I was struck by the title of an early album by Lady Gaga: *'Born This Way'*. I believe this title speaks to us on several levels. The first level goes back to when we first heard this expression as small children, when our mother told us not to make fun of or stare at a handicapped person, because 'they did not choose to be that way; they were born that way'. I think Lady Gaga is tapping into this understanding. She is saying 'If my outfits strike you as odd, or my videos offend you, well, you can't make fun or criticize me. I didn't choose to be this way, I was born this way. I thus had no choice about it; it was a gift or a fate to which I was condemned.' I think, however, there is also a second message behind the first understanding, and this is more aggressive or defiant: 'the most important thing a person can do is to bring their hidden essence to the surface for all to see, that is, to transfer this interior core to the light of day, out in the open, through an act of self-expansion, actualization or fulfillment. Thus, not only is what I am doing not wrong, it is emphatically right; in fact, it is what we *all* should be doing. *Not* to do so would a moral flaw, a reneging on a moral obligation. The supreme moral obligation in fact, to which all others should be subordinated, is to bring this inner core to expression, to the surface, to make it exterior and public. Hence the title, 'Expressive Individualism'. Anything else shows a lack of courage or resolve.

This can take a less attractive form. In September, 2011, in the US Open Tennis Championships at Flushing Meadows, NY, Serena Williams was playing Samantha Stosur of Australia in the women's finals. Serena lost the first set and was falling behind in the second. When she at last hit a strong forehand she gave a celebratory shout, but was deducted a point for having disturbed her opponent's concentration before the point was over. She was furious; when she ended up losing the game, at the change-over she verbally abused the umpire, who was a lady from Greece. She was then given a code violation. According to the paper, her response was: 'Code violation? I expressed who I am. This is America, last time I checked.'

I'm not picking Serena Williams out from the crowd, but rather taking her to be representative of a much wider group. I would suggest that whenever any of us feels embarrassed by a form of behavior, and can see no other way out, we fall back on some form of expressive individualism as a way of deflecting criticism and exonerating ourselves. We resort to a series of one-liners or sound-bites such as 'It felt natural', or 'It seemed like a good idea at the time'. This has become our go-to ethic when we are in a jam, under stress or simply want to exculpate ourselves from questionable behavior. I think it is also significant that Serena identified America as the country where this ethic has become an unspoken law of the land that needs no further justification. As Frank Sinatra sang, America is a wonderful country because here each of us can do things 'my way'. The suggestion is that there is no 'right' or 'wrong' way to do something, there is only 'your way'. Consequences are of small importance; it almost doesn't matter if you hurt someone. Authentically expressing yourself has become the last holdout and redoubt for the sacred, the only route the 'noumenal' dimension has for boring a channel into the 'phenomenal' world and creating value. As long as you can say you were 'expressing yourself'—doing things 'your way' - you cannot be criticized. It's like a 'get out of jail free' card in Monopoly. Sinatra's version of 'My Way' has become the most requested 'hymn' to be played in crematoria world-wide as a deceased's body disappears behind the curtain or into the fiery furnace. In waving good-bye, my final act is to exonerate myself; in effect, I play 'God' and grant myself absolution.[2]

Where did this lifestyle come from? Did it fall from the skies, or appear like a mushroom one morning, with nobody knowing where it came from? Or can we identify an historical event that served as a precedent for what is now widespread and passes without comment?

Before there was Elvis, there was Lord Byron. Before there was John Updike or Seamus Heaney, there was William Wordsworth. Before there was William Faulkner, there was Samuel Taylor Coleridge. Before there was the generals Patton, Montgomery and MacArthur, there was Napoleon,

Wellington and Lord Nelson. Before there was Jimmy Hendrix and Eric Clapton, there was Beethoven and Mozart. Before there was J. D. Salinger, there was Johann Wolfgang von Goethe. In short, there was a Romantic revolt. In line with the Enlightenment criticism of the feudal nobility as useless, corrupt and oppressive, and Rousseau's revolutionary declaration of the 'rights of man', there was a call for a new 'nobility' based on egalitarian values of liberty and the recognition of natural merit. Napoleon burst on the scene as the iconic Romantic hero, because he succeeded in destroying one world—the *Ancien Régime* of kings and nobles—and creating another—the Republic—in extending the scope and ideals of the French Revolution to all of Europe. Byron modeled himself on Napoleon; he died fighting for the liberation of Greece against the Turks. The Brontë sisters popularized the Byronic hero through the characters of Heathcliff in *Wuthering Heights* and Mr. Rochester in *Jane Eyre*, through which he has become a central icon in hundreds of novels—the so-called 'Gothic novel'—and later the movies and television. Napoleon and Milton were the twin engines who succeeded in launching the English Romantics; Napoleon's revolutionary politics had to be lifted into the artistic sphere, while Milton's towering authority and indomitable power had to be similarly directed towards a revolutionary artistic, rather than a theological agenda. There is an interesting return of the Romantic hero towards its Luciferian root in Bram Stoker's turn-of-the-century *Dracula*. Like all Romantic heroes, Dracula is a vessel of smoldering masculinity—dark, brooding, handsome—but he is also a vampire. He preys on human beings, and turns them into vampires as well. At the height of the scandal against Byron for incest and 'unspeakable cruelty in marriage', he was described by his supporter Francis Jeffrey as a 'ruined archangel'.

Our culture is, for better or worse, a Romantic culture, indeed, a revolutionary culture, that is one predicated on the rejection of neo-classical restrictions. And the gem, the diamond in the center of the Romantic revolt is the figure of the artistic genius. He is the engine that makes this movement go, he is the essential foundation on which the revolution is predicated. During the Renaissance, Georgio Vasari (1511-74) was the first to identify the poet as a hero, with particular reference to Michelangelo's *David*. It was Goethe, however, who first presented the poet as a hero in a work of literature (*Torquato Tasso*, 1790); this changed the way artists were seen and honored. Thomas Carlyle adopted Goethe's innovation in his work *On Heroes, Hero-worship, and the Heroic in History* (1841).

Genius is a central topic in German academic philosophy from Emmanuel Kant to Arthur Schopenhauer. German culture, from Lessing's 1766 manifesto in his *Laocoön*, defines itself as 'Romantic', against the previously dominant French neo-classicism of Corneille, Racine and Moliere coming out of Versailles. But where did the idea of 'artistic genius' come from? What was its source, and what does it really refer to? To answer these questions we must take one step further back. We must return to Milton's *Paradise Lost*.

Milton is so great a poet, however, that one should perhaps hesitate and think twice before one puts him in the dock or dares include him as part of—indeed, the center of—this tradition. On the other hand, Shakespeare warns us of the need for courage at such moments when official pressure and authority would deter us from the direction conscience pushes us to examine in order to uncover the origin of a problem. It is rather at such moments that we should redouble our efforts:

> Why, man, he doth bestride the narrow world
> Like a colossus, and we petty men
> Walk under his huge legs, and peep about
> To find ourselves dishonorable graves.
> Men at some time are masters of their fates;
> The fault, dear Brutus, is not in our stars,
> But in ourselves, that we are underlings.
> *Julius Caesar*, 2,1
> Thus conscience does make cowards of us all,
> And thus the native hue of resolution
> Is sickled o'er with the pale cast of thought.
> And enterprises of great pith and moment —
> With this regard their currents turn awry
> And lose the name of action.
> *Hamlet* 3, 1

Paradise Lost, published in 1667, is famously described by Samuel Johnson as 'a poem which, considered with respect to design may claim the first place, and with respect to performance the second, among the productions of the human mind.' However, the design is not what we would expect; rather, the performance is all. The poem begins with the rebel angels at their lowest point, cast into hell and stunned after the failure of their rebellion, from which dizzying confusion Satan - with undiminished strength and unrepentant—announces the fight is not over and seeks to rouse his fellow devils to greater ardor:

> not for those,
> Nor what the Potent Victor in his rage
> Can else inflict, do I repent or change,
> Though chang'd in outward lustre; that fixt mind
> And high disdain, from sence of injur'd merit,
> That with the mightiest rais'd me to contend,
> And to the fierce contention brought along
> Innumerable force of Spirits arm'd
> That durst dislike his reign, and me preferring,
> His utmost power with adverse power oppos'd
> In dubious Battel on the Plains of Heav'n,
> And shook his throne. What though the field be lost?
> All is not lost; the unconquerable Will,
> And study of revenge, immortal hate,
> And courage never to submit or yield:
> And what is else not to be overcome?
> That Glory never shall his wrath or might
> Extort from me. . .
> through experience of this great event
> In Arms not worse, in foresight much advanc't,
> We may with more successful hope resolve
> To wage by force or guile eternal Warr
> Irreconcileable, to our grand Foe,
> Who now triumphs, and in th' excess of joy
> Sole reigning

It is interesting that the book of Genesis does not mention a revolt by the angels. We have only a one-line reference in the last book in the Bible, the Book of Revelation (Rev. 12: 7-9), to the archangel Michael 'casting the dragon out of heaven.' It was the Greek Fathers of the early Church, chiefly Origen and Irenaeus, who developed the story of Lucifer to explain where

The Devil Made Me Do It: How the West Disguised its Diabolical Switch of Messiah

devils came from. God did not create devils, so where *did* they come from?

'Lucifer' as a name arises in the Old Testament as a term of mockery by the prophets Isaiah and Ezekiel to tease and make fun of the upstart king of Babylon, who in their view has dared to rival God, and thus, like the 'morning star' which rises too high, must eventually plummet in humiliating defeat:

> 'How art thou fallen from heaven, O Lucifer, son of the morning? How art thou cut down to the ground, which didst weaken the nations!
>
> For thou hast said in thine heart, I will ascend into heaven, I will exult my throne above the stars of God. I will sit also upon the mount of the congregation, in the sides of the north:
>
> I will ascend above the heights of the clouds, I will be like the most High. Yet thou shalt be brought down to hell, to the sides of the pit.' Ezekiel 14:12-15

This pattern supplied a template for overweening pride being brought to a humiliating reversal that the Church Fathers reached back to to explain the many devils the gospels depict Jesus casting out.

Merging with ecumenical neo-Platonic philosophy, the story developed was that Lucifer was the highest creature, the most powerful, intelligent and beautiful of the arch-angels, until the Father revealed to him his plan to send his Son into the world to redeem humanity from their sins. The Son would have a human nature which would automatically become the highest creature, because it was suited to be joined to divinity. This would demote Lucifer to the second spot. Lucifer's pride prevented him from accepting this plan; he would not bend the knee to Jesus. He rebels, takes some angels with him; there is a 'celestial combat' with Michael and the loyal angels. Michael prevails and casts Lucifer out of heaven, whereupon he becomes 'Satan' in hell, who will spend all eternity trying to sabotage Jesus' plan of human redemption.

This is the story Milton inherited, but in *Paradise Lost* he makes several changes—many trivial, some more important. Trivially, in Milton's version Lucifer is defeated not by Michael, but by the Son Himself, the second person of the Trinity; there is no real contest, for no one can fight God, who is the source of power. But Lucifer's battle is not over; as indicated in the quotation above, he has not given up, but will search for an alternative form of retaliation and will rise to new heights of hatred and revenge.

Another change is that, after the fall of Adam and Eve, for Milton we are saved not by the passion, death and resurrection of Jesus (Milton has little patience for these traditional sentimentalities) but rather by the debate, competition and final rejection of the temptations to which Jesus is subjected by Satan *before* his Galilean ministry has even begun. Milton was a life-long controversialist and the chief propagandist for the Puritan cause; the forensic exchange of Jesus with Satan appealed to Milton as a keen debater. In the synoptic gospels, after Jesus is baptized by John the Baptist, he withdraws into the wilderness to fast for forty days, after which he is tempted. These temptations consist in three promises of ever greater power, if Jesus will only prostrate himself before Satan and worship him. In Milton's version, if Jesus had succumbed to this temptation, Satan planned to cast him down from the great height, thereby destroying his human nature; instead, however, Jesus resists the temptation and casts Satan down! Hence the line in scripture: 'I saw Satan fall from heaven' (Luke 10:18). Milton interprets this to mean that Satan's reign is over, and we are now saved! The rest of the gospel is a 'mopping up' operation; the essential victory was secured at the very beginning, *before* Jesus' preaching and teaching mission had even begun. Milton is not even sure there *is* a Resurrection; in any case, it's not needed, for we are saved by Jesus' victory in this first contest in scripture-quotation and forensic jousting. This novel soteriology corresponds to that of no known Christian denomination; as C. S. Lewis noted, Milton belonged to a Church with only one member—himself.

The most serious change, however, is that - in his hatred for his rival Jesus - Milton's Lucifer rejects not only Jesus as the highest creature, he rejects the Father as father. The Father's decision is felt by Lucifer to be so callous, heavy or unfair, the Father himself so arbitrary and inadequate that there is no alternative but to remove Him entirely—to deny, reject or effectively kill him off—for Lucifer to announce that he has fathered *himself*. Milton thereby inflates Lucifer's rebellion, he heightens Lucifer's alienation and radicalizes his estrangement in a breath-taking manner to an infinite degree. In effect, he denies his creaturely status. In book five of *Paradise Lost* Satan is reminding his fellow devils of the grounds for their rebellion and responds as follows to an objection from the loyal angel Abdiel:

> 'That we were formd then saist thou? & the work
> Of secondarie hands, by task transferd
> From Father to his Son? strange point and new!
> When this creation was? rememberst thou
> Thy making, while the Maker gave thee being?
> We know no time when we were not as now;
> Know none before us, self-begot, self-rais'd
> By our own quick'ning power, when fatal course
> Had circl'd his full Orbe, the birth mature
> Of this our native Heav'n, Ethereal Sons.
> Our puissance is our own, our own right hand
> Shall teach us highest deeds, by proof to try
> Who is our equal'.Bk. 5, 854-866

This announcement confounds the understanding. How can a creature—indeed, the most intelligent of creatures—presume to make such a claim? This is the first time *in all of Western literature* that a creature has dared pronounce such words. This is the blasphemy of blasphemies, a heresy so deep there is no name for it: a creature declaring itself to be equal to God.

Milton gets away with it by putting it in the mouth of a devil; this way he can exploit and profit from its provocative potential for his poetic drama while at the same time washing his hands of any responsibility. After all, it is a demon who is speaking this way. Still, this tactic is shocking, dangerous and risky. Had such been written a hundred years earlier, Milton would likely have been burned at the stake, by Catholics and Protestants alike. So why did he write it?

Milton had a problem. He was Oliver Cromwell's Latin secretary, fighting on the Puritan side in the English Civil War against King Charles I, but also against monarchy *per se*; he wanted no more kings. At the same time, he is writing a poem about the Prince of Heaven rebelling against the

King of Heaven; are we surprised that one influenced the other? Milton *invests in* Lucifer; in fact, he *identifies* with Lucifer. Lucifer is his stand-in in the poem. This accounts for the outsized vehemence of his emotion, his indomitability and the unquenchable quality of his rage. Intuitively Milton encourages Lucifer, he roots him on, he wants him to succeed. Milton coined the phrase 'injured merit' for this sentiment—one of thousands of expressions he gave the English language. Lucifer felt he *deserved* to be the highest creature; it was unfair for the Father to advance Jesus above him. Milton is doing the same thing against the earthly king that Lucifer is doing against the heavenly king; Milton uses the poem as an *apologia* for his own (similarly failed) rebellion. In spite of their common disaster, he holds that the revolt was justified—for the cause was *just*. When serious issues are at stake, it is more noble to go out 'with head bloody but unbowed' than to accept in mute cowardice a shameful travesty and betrayal of that justice.

From his formation in Renaissance neo-classical style Milton inherited an antipathy to the 'barbarism' of scholastic philosophy and theology and an opposition to the clerical 'tyranny' of the Roman Church, but he initially accommodated the risky Anglican experiment of a union between Church and State. However, with time and negative experience his sensibility expanded and his irritability overflowed, first against the Anglican divorce laws, then against the Presbyterian attempt to steal the Puritan victory after the Civil War. Finally, he ended (like William Blake) in turning against divine authority altogether, favoring Lucifer in his rebellion against God, in his final self-exonerating *apologia pro vita sua*. In an unprecedented, heretical burst of creativity, Lucifer is substituted as the new Messiah.

Several critics have pointed out that, because of his sense of betrayal by a cosmic fate and consequent *agon*, Satan is structurally the 'hero' of *Paradise Lost*. Dramatically he is by far the most interesting, powerful and arresting figure, more so than God the Father, who is not seen, as well as Jesus, Adam and Eve. The poem begins with the defeated and exhausted devils landing in Hell after the failure of their rebellion. This would remind any English reader of the decimated condition of the defeated Puritan leaders upon the restoration of the Stuart monarchy with Charles II in 1660. Despite their failure, after Satan's urging the devils begin plotting to sabotage the Father's attempt at a new creation of human beings after the

The Devil Made Me Do It: How the West Disguised its Diabolical Switch of Messiah

disappointing results with the angels; this is Milton's subliminal signal to his readers that the Puritans neither can nor should give up as well, nor accept their defeat as final. Satan's undiminished resolve and fury are manifest in the several later occasions where he encounters devils who realize how much they have lost and consequently are having second thoughts about the wisdom of continuing the rebellion. Satan at such moments repristinates the sting of the original offense; he refreshes their pique and re-ignites their sputtering indignation. He rehearses magnificently the cosmic injustice that functions as the pretext and justification for their revolt, re-combusting their flagging irritation. These are the moments when he waxes most eloquent, producing the descending cascades of sulphurous, crushing denunciation and furious, character-moulding poetry; as some have suggested, psychologically speaking, the plot exists as an excuse for Milton's triumphal presentation of Satan, rather than Satan as a support for the poem. His resentment does not tire, the fire of his supernal outrage is never tamped, his vertiginous anger cannot be assuaged. A spirit of *saevum indignatio* infuses the whole poem and accounts for its fascination, if only to answer the question 'Can he really get away with this?'

Indeed, Milton's Lucifer is the model for most later expressions of such supernal contempt and rejection in English literature and drama. As we can today x-ray or scan old paintings to discover an earlier scene on the canvas below the one painted above, Milton uses the traditional story of the Fall as a palimpsest to cover, conceal, yet also retain and effectively communicate, an opposing narrative lodged beneath, one that comes through ideologically and emotionally loud and clear. This is the implicit communication, the 'subliminal message' of the poem—that goes *against* its apparent or surface consolation. *Paradise Lost* is not a traditional reminder of man's 'Fall' and the ruination of his vocation to greatness—exactly the opposite. The heretical message rather is that God the Father—like all tyrants—because he is opposed to such greatness, must be toppled and overthrown. For later poets, a rhetorical door is opened; a new, previously forbidden example is installed. Acting like Satan becomes permissible, for advanced spirits, it becomes a challenge, incentive and model—henceforth a presumed literary reference that diffuses its own ideological permission. It doesn't change the relative score; it changes the game.

The poem is transmuted into an account, not of Original Sin, but of 'Original Right'—the right of the creative artist to overthrow all authorities who attempt to contain, censor or stifle the full expression of his powers. William Blake, whose bizarre mythology also turns against the Christian God (Urizen), caught the scent early when he wrote that in *Paradise Lost*, Milton is 'a great poet, and of the devil's party without knowing it'. In other words, whatever he says on the surface, or whatever faults he finds with Satan, an identification is nonetheless established that is instinctive, involuntary, pre-conscious and automatic. By his unforgettable depiction of Satan, Milton exposes his own state of mind. We are warranted in paying attention to this unnerving depiction because a like tower of distemper is, for example, strangely but conspicuously absent from the other great influence on English literature, the plays of Shakespeare. King Lear goes mad raging on the moors at imagined ingratitude, and becomes like a child, rewarding the daughters who flatter him the most. Iago's hatred of Othello is hidden, secretive and probably to be explained through a combination of competition, jealousy and resentment. Otherwise, rivalries and contests are measured and proportionate, unlike the titanic, unassuageable fire of Milton's Satan.

Two hundred years later the Romantic poets Lord Bryon, Wordsworth, Keats, Shelly and Coleridge reached back to before neo-classical figures such as John Dryden, Alexander Pope and John Milton. Unlike the neo-classical poets, Milton had the power to touch the emotions of awe, fascination and danger—the Romantic 'sublime'. They fed especially on his depiction of Lucifer: like Lucifer, the Romantic poet is in rebellion against the neo-classical unities, the strictures on poetic form and content; like Lucifer, the Romantic poet forcefully rejects the cultural role of a servile ornament within a hierarchical system. He disdains the horizontal supports from royal or aristocratic patronage or from a bourgeois audience he disdains as philistine. The Romantic poets transferred Milton's novel portrait of Lucifer from the angelic to the human realm, to fashion the new portrait of the artist as genius; that is, they secularized Milton's revised angelology. Because of the legacy and powerful influence of this poem, for the past four hundred years our culture is most accurately described as 'Luciferian'. Lucifer figures explicitly in Byron's poem *Cain, a Mystery*

The Devil Made Me Do It: How the West Disguised its Diabolical Switch of Messiah

(1821), and Satan in *The Vision of Judgment* (1822). Shelley died in 1822 at age 29. In his posthumously published essay '*On the Devil and Devils*', he muses:

> 'Milton gives the Devil all imaginable advantage; and the arguments with which he exposes the injustice and impotent weakness of his adversary, are such as, had they been printed, distinct from the shelter of any dramatic order, would have been answered by the most conclusive of syllogisms—persecution. As it is, *Paradise Lost* has conferred on the modern mythology a systematic form; and when the immeasurable and unceasing mutability of time shall have added one more superstition to those which have already arisen and decayed upon the earth, commentators and critics will be learnedly employed in elucidating the religion of ancestral Europe, only not utterly forgotten because it will have participated in the eternity of genius. The Devil owes everything to Milton. Dante and Tasso present us with a very gross idea of him. Milton divested him of a sting, hoof, and horns, and clothed him with the sublime grandeur of a graceful but tremendous spirit.'

The English tradition was not alone in moving in this direction. In *Dichtung und Wahrheit* (1811), Goethe advances an attempt to retain belief in the goodness of God against a recognition of substantial evil in creation (such as the Lisbon earthquake of 1755). He does this, however, through the unorthodox theory that God had entrusted the creation of the world not to his Son, but to Lucifer (Collected Works, IV, 261f.) This disturbing doctrine had also been part of the earlier Cathars' (or Albigensian) heresy. It provides a handy solution to the problem of accounting for the surprising amount of evil in God's world; indeed, the difficulty then switches to accounting for the puzzling presence of good in a world created by the devil. Accepting Spinoza's naturalistic monism, once we recognize the predetermined fate this God has fixed for us, we have a choice only between affirming joyfully this fate to be good in a dogmatic but Pickwickian sense, or of recognizing evil honestly to be evil, and falling into melancholy. A Nietzschean 'Become what thou art!' is the only consistent (and inescapable) destiny. We serve God, not by worshiping Him as a separate being, but by imitating Him by developing into points of creation which consistently recognize—and take refuge within—their oneness with this divine core.

Milton's transgressive move, however, proved too bold. Even his close Romantic followers soon fell back to the less shocking figure of Prometheus, as a rebel against cosmic injustice who would have a chance of cultural acceptance. It was too heretical or out of bounds to nominate Lucifer as a cultural hero for the theologically conservative English population. When the heightened aesthetic mood had passed and the poetic reader had returned to sobriety, it was unrealistic to propose Lucifer as an ideal. Percy Shelley's masterwork, *Prometheus Unbound,* presents itself as a re-writing of *Paradise Lost*, with Prometheus carefully substituted for Lucifer as a classical inspiration and more orthodox justification for artistic genius. In its preface Shelley writes:

> 'The only imaginary being, resembling in any degree Prometheus, is Satan; and Prometheus is, in my judgment, a more poetical character than Satan, because, in addition to courage, and majesty, and firm and patient opposition to omnipotent force, he is susceptible of being described as exempt from the taints of ambition, envy, revenge, and a desire for personal aggrandizement, which, in the hero of *Paradise Lost*, interfere with the interest. The character of Satan engenders in the mind a pernicious casuistry which leads us to weigh his faults with his wrongs, and to excuse the former because the latter exceed all measure. In the minds of those who consider that magnificent fiction with a religious feeling it engenders something worse. But Prometheus is, as it were, the type of the highest perfection of moral and intellectual nature, impelled by the purest and the truest motives to the best and noblest ends.'[3]

Faced with such strenuous opposition, Shelley falls back to a milder, less disruptive version of Milton's thesis. Prometheus is a 'sanitized' version of Lucifer, with the offending traits washed out; he retains for Shelley, however, enough similarity to transmit the same Romantic protest. In *Prometheus Unbound,* the artist-as-genius has shed his diabolic ancestry and heretical associations to assume an acceptable classical magnificence to lead humanity to liberation from an unfair and equally tyrannical high god and equally repressive created order. Prometheus steals fire from heaven for mankind's benefit; Jupiter chains him to a rock to punish him for his disobedience. In contrast to Aeschylus' handling, however, in Shelley's version Prometheus refuses to apologize or show any remorse for his crime, and at the conclusion Prometheus and the godhead are not reconciled.[4] Such a refusal to submit to a deity now routinely depicted as unjust becomes a conspicuous and recurring theme in contemporary re-appropriations of traditional tales, as when Goethe scandalously has Faust rescued for Heaven and evading the Hell to which he had been justly condemned, down to Sartre's *The Flies* and Camus's *The Myth of Sisyphus*.

The Greek goal of excellence in craftsmanship was '*areté*', a species of 'the good'; it had much to do with training, practice and patience, which must shape, augment and complement native talent. This applied across the arts and crafts; a sculptor or a painter was considered much like a carpenter or a plumber. He would attach himself to a master and his workshop and progress through a series of stages until he earned his license and then had the right to set himself up as an independent craftsman. Depending on his skill and industry, commissions might then come in. In the Romantic period, however, the artist gravitates towards the epithet of 'genius'. The traditional vocation of art as mimetic—from the Greek word for imitation, of either the Platonic Form or the singular individual—is undermined or called into question; on the contrary, the artist now delights in being described as original and creative. This is no longer intended as a euphemism or metaphor: he rather brings into being something that has *never existed before*. As William Blake put it in *Jerusalem*:

> I must create a system or be enslaved by another man's;
> I will not reason and compare; my business is to create.

The Romantic experience was never better expressed than by Robert Browning in his poem *Abt Vogler*:

> And I know not, save in this, such gift be allowed to man
> That out of three sounds he frame, not a fourth sound, but a star.

He thereby usurps the place of God; he has effectively killed the Father. With Lucifer he declares 'I know none before me; I am self-begot.' [5]

This agonal competition for dominance has become central to contemporary poetry. According to Harold Bloom, each Romantic poet begins his career with a feeling of having come late to this competition, and of being condemned to marginality and insignificance by the great works of his predecessors. He is spurred by an 'anxiety of influence' or threat of definitive inferior status, to achieve 'anteriority' over his predecessors by increasing the radicality of his revolt, reaching a closer proximity to the Romantic sublime, and by his own 'transumptive' or upheaving achievement, turning the tables, reversing the direction of influence, thereby banishing his intimidating precursors to the marginality and oblivion from which he initially suffered. He tries to eclipse and replace his predecessors in the common Romantic competition—to become *the* artistic genius. By this achievement he denies, rejects and 'kills' the Father, John Milton, who inspired the entire Romantic rebellion. He also rejects or kills the later 'fathers'—his own siblings, chicks from the same nest—leaving only himself.

Those familiar with the works of René Girard and his theory of mimetic desire will recognize how Girard's theory fits hand in glove with Bloom's account. For Girard we desire what we witness others desiring; that is, our desires do not naturally have a specific object but rather are underdetermined and plastic, so as to become socially molded. Once a youngster catches sight of what older children value and desire, he comes to value and desire the same for himself, setting off a rivalrous competition that rises to ever-higher levels until violence breaks out. This is also true for adults. For Girard, this is the origin of 'culture' in every proto-human society; the only hominids who survived are those who serendipitously discovered the 'scapegoat' mechanism, whereby this violence that otherwise leads to a 'war of all against all' and threatens the entire group with destruction, is narrowed and directed instead towards a marginal figure who is somehow odd or different, and who can for this reason be held responsible for the disturbance that currently afflicts the group. The execution and elimination of this scapegoat allows the group to return to its peaceful condition. At this point the individual who at first was indicted as a villain is exalted as a savior who by his death has overcome violence and has reconciled the potentially violent forces within the group. He is worshiped as a god, and his self-sacrifice and subsequent apotheosis are repeated as a regular ritual whenever mimetic rivalry threatens again to disturb the group. According to Bloom, such rivalrous competition defines the relation of the Romantic poets one to another, each one stimulated by the daunting achievement of his predecessors, and by his own strenuous efforts, seeking to banish these precursors to the marginality and insignificance he himself experienced.

What Bellah and Taylor call 'expressive individualism' represents a democratization and universalization of this transformation of the artist into a genius now to the population at large, or, moving from the other direction, the claim by the general population to share in the privileges and higher status hitherto reserved for this quasi-distinct species. We assist at an 'ontological inflation' of human nature, a spread of the Romantic rebellion from an elite few to the masses in general. We are thereby encouraged to press *our* claim to a concealed divine status, and by our performance and attitude, to render this status no longer hidden or secret. We now can each say, 'I know none before me, I am self-begot.'

To recapitulate: When the Father becomes sufficiently inadequate, when he imposes a burden we esteem too heavy or unfair to accept, the only appropriate response is to remove or kill him. This response is prefigured and licensed by the portrait Milton gives of Lucifer in *Paradise Lost*. It is then transferred from the angelic realm to the human during the Romantic movement through the medium of the artist as genius, and finally has become democratized and universalized in our time as the ethic of 'expressive individualism.' To the extent that we embrace 'expressive individualism' as the default lifestyle of our time, we are implicitly committed to Milton's Lucifer as the archetype for human fulfillment or self-realization, which I believe to be a toxic model. This not only transforms a previously heretical comportment and disruptive conduct into a now-tolerated behavior, it unveils and proclaims this as the no-longer-secret ideal of human development. In an inversion of the West's traditional set of primary symbols, what was previously the deepest and most offensive blasphemy is installed and spelled out as orthodoxy. We have used the artist-as-genius to disguise our switch of Messiah from Jesus to Lucifer. In a clever and covert terrorist raid on the religious temple, not only is an astounding desecration committed, but this diabolical reversal has subtly insinuated itself as the *new creed* of the community.

Notes

[1] Although it is dated now, Harvard professor Irving Babbitt's *Rousseau and Romanticism* (Houghton Mifflin 1919; reprinted by Transaction Publishers, London/New Brunswick, 2009) is valuable for having collected most of the relevant texts on the cult of the 'genius' from both well-known and lesser-known sources from this period. This cult was all-pervasive, the centre of the Romantic ideology and now part of the cultural 'weather' - as it still is by default or lack of anything to replace it, but now also in popular culture. There has been a 'trickle down' effect of this unique resource to calm status anxieties by making it available to everyone, and thus more universal or democratic; geniuses are no longer rare or an 'elite'. We can all be 'geniuses' - in the right context.

[2] The animated film *Frozen*, with its signature song 'Let It Go', also gives powerful expression to 'expressive individualism'. The latter is a staple in American stage and screen, from Scarlett O'Hara's words 'I will never be hungry again' at the end of *Gone with the Wind*, to the musicals *Golden Rainbow* ('I've gotta be me') to tongue in cheek in *Camelot* ('C'est moi, c'est moi'), to *Funny Girl* ('Don't Rain on My Parade').

[3] Shelly, Percy Bysshe, *Prometheus Unbound, A Lyrical Drama in Four Acts with Other Poems*, London, C and J Ollier, 1820, pp. viii-ix.

[4] Lucifer was a focal reference for all the Romantic artists. Thomas De Quincey once made an offhand but telling allusion to Wordsworth, to whom he was initially in thrall, as surprisingly a model for Lucifer, rather than the other way around: 'Never describe Wordsworth as equal in pride to Lucifer. No, but if you have occasion to write a life of Lucifer, set down that by possibility, in respect to pride, he might be some type of Wordsworth.' Cited in *Guilty Thing,* by Francis Wilson. Mary Shelly subtitled her novel *Frankenstein*: 'A Modern Prometheus'.

[5] Paul Collier and John Kay, in their book *Greed is Dead: Politics After Individualism* (Allen Lane, 2020), have further refined Expressive Individualism, arguing first as economists not that 'Greed is good' but rather bad, culminating recently in the greed for attention characteristic of narcissistic celebrities, protesters and digital warriors eager to declare their

moral superiority and be judged 'by the intensity of passion rather than the depth of knowledge'. This leads to a split between 'elite individualists' on the left and 'possessive individualists' of market fundamentalism on the right. Both promote the new 'politics of grievances' whose extremists have hijacked the main political parties, keeping them from their principal job of focusing on community and a practical pursuit of shared goals. He thereby usurps the place of God; he has effectively killed the Father. With Lucifer he declares 'I know none before me; I am self-begot'.

Chapter 6

The Sorrow That Dares Not Say Its Name; The Inadequate Father, the Motor of History

Although the following essay is literary-philosophical, it arose from a practical interest. I have been struck by how widespread today is the complaint about the 'inadequate father'. Of course, a father may be inadequate in diverse ways, either absconding, absent and weak, or overbearing, bullying and tyrannical, or some combination of these. Further, I am not restricting the term 'father' to its narrow biological sense, but using it rather as a metaphor for any institution or structure which an individual or a group feels should have been in place to guide, direct and protect them in important situations, but did not do its job properly. Consequently, they are willing to concede that they are not all they could have been, but they insist it is not their fault, rather the fault of the 'father' who should have done his job better. This ties in with the fashionable appeal of 'victimhood'. Everybody today seems to want to cast themselves as a 'victim', for reasons similar to those mentioned above. If you are a 'victim', then there must be an 'oppressor'– and some 'parent' organization that should have guided, directed and protected you against the oppressor, but again did not do its job adequately. It is striking how many individuals and groups around the world today choose to perceive themselves, and to present themselves to others, as 'victims'; it has indeed become a preferred characterization of our age, for it carries with it a rhetorical advantage that trumps all others. If you are able to cast yourself as a 'victim', and have others accept this, you disarm and neutralize criticism, not only of what you are, but of what you are currently doing—because the latter can be presented as a just 'compensation' for what you have suffered. As with guilt, there is no built-in quota or statute of limitations. This rhetoric was not as common thirty or forty years ago.

There is an added factor here in America and the New World generally where, according to a whispered criticism, as our ancestors crossed the ocean, they experienced a 'drop in civilization'. Life here was initially without some of the structures and institutions which had evolved over thousands of years in the Old World, which could thus be presumed there but were absent here. As we won with difficulty our independence, we unconsciously repudiated much of the 'higher culture' of the colonial master, throwing out the baby with the bathwater. As the 'economic bubble' of having won the Second World War has gradually dissipated, we have discovered that we are handicapped by an absence of the forms of maturation and self-realization that arise in and are necessary for dealing with prolonged peace. In our 'ideology of liberty', our adults become essentially grown children, unschooled in anything higher, and thus have particular difficulty assuming the responsibilities of parenthood. They are forced to fall back upon a military style of giving orders, because on this side of the water, 'final causes' in the form of commonly admired or agreed on goals for striving are not in place. In this sense there is an absence of the 'adequate father'. Further, as 'American Culture' expands through publicity and the media, we spread the same disease.

There is another relevant factor, the 'celebrity-liberationist' lifestyle that has been diffused into the general population since the 1960s and has become a default secular ethic of our time, replacing the traditional Judeo-Christian decalogue. The former is invoked as a justification for aggressively seeking fame and fortune, and making no attempt to conceal this; rather than worrying that such an attitude will cause offense, it is worn proudly and defiantly in the hope that others will identify with it, thereby branding the performer a cultural hero. This popular strategy towards fulfillment itself rests on a metaphysic of 'expressive individualism', a position that holds that the supreme ethical imperative to which other obligations must be subordinated is for each to bring forward their hidden noumenal core, the only source of value, into phenomenal appearances where it may be admired and such that creation will for the first time be complete. This change in Western culture made possible by greater affluence and security represents a trickle-down phenomenon and democratization of the awe reserved for the artist revered as a genius during the nineteenth century, now spread to the entire population. Anything that constrains this expansion, which interrupts or limits this transfer, is to be rejected as parental abuse, psychological repression or cultural imperialism.

The theme of the inadequate father finds its *locus classicus* in the Bible in the story of David and his son Absolom. Absolom has a sister, Tamar, and a half-brother Amnon. Amnon rapes Tamar. Absolom waits two full years for his father David to do something, but David does nothing. Absolom then kills Amnon himself and flees to his relatives. David could still reach him there, but again does nothing. Absolom stays away three years until finally 'the heart of the king went out, yearning for Absolom; for he was now consoled over the death of Amnon' (II Sam 13:37–39). Absolom feels disgust for his father; David's yearning for Absolom is derived, beyond parental love, from guilt and self-loathing at his own lack of action. He cannot bring himself to confess this to Absolom, however, even though it is he who wants to be forgiven. When David finally admits Absolom into his presence after five years absence, all he can do is kiss him wordlessly. Absolom has done what David should have done, and David recognizes this; Absolom is the man David should have been, and is not. Although Absolom is officially the criminal, he is the morally superior. In this instance David is a coward, and wants to be allowed to *remain* a coward—and remain king! Absolom cannot accept this and rebels against his father. When David learns that against his orders Absolom has been killed in battle, he disgraces and humiliates himself by wailing all night in the presence of his troops, who then slink home as though they had lost rather than won.

Platonism is many things, but one thing that Platonism always involves is a commitment to Forms. That is, the plausibility of Platonism is tied to the plausibility of archetypes as a philosophical hypothesis. There seems to be an age factor at work in the acceptance or rejection of archetypes; philosophy in one of its meanings is the wisdom born of experience, and as you get more experience the power of an archetype grows on you. When we are young, we distrust received stereotypes and often express our rebellion with a rabid empiricism that is happy to upset what is perceived as a simplistic and complacent conservatism. It has been said only partially in jest that as young people we are empiricists and Epicureans, in middle age we mature into Aristotelians and finally in old age we subside into stuffy and boring Platonists.

There is something to this. With greater experience, and different types of experience, there is simply no denying the power of an archetype to organize and integrate our knowledge; grandfathers see further than fathers, and fathers further than sons. It comes down to the difference between having to interpret reality from a snapshot, or being able to avail yourself of a many-reeled motion picture. What seems implausible or far-fetched to a young person becomes obvious, even ruefully inescapable to the older eye. Older people perceive the oak tree in the acorn, and they look for the signs of character behind the glow of youth. When you are old, the stones themselves have mouths, because in what concerns the world around us, it didn't used to be this way. What youth takes to be fixed and permanent, old age knows is recent and fragile. Hearing the approach of death, old age invests what little it has left in things that will last, realizing that most things don't.

Readers of Plato's *Dialogues* agree that some of the most beautiful passages occur in *The Symposium*, the evening of drinking where each participant gives a speech in praise of love. The last and most elaborate is that of Socrates, who recounts a series of instructions he received from Diotima of Mantineia that take the dialogue, and Plato's philosophy, to its most lofty heights. Early on we are told that love is the desire to make copies of the beautiful—to give 'birth in beauty, whether of body or of soul'. This is the deepest human desire, the underlying human desire, for which one risks death and to which one subordinates all else, for by one's legacy one attains a kind of immortality, and one tries to make one's legacy as beautiful as possible. In other words, even when we don't know we are doing it, *this* is what we are doing, this is what we are *really* doing; there is some sort of an identity between the 'is' and the 'ought' in Diotima's instruction. If you can take this illumination on board, you return to your normal pursuits with new eyes. You scrutinize your activities against this proposed criterion. The lesson is, since you are pursuing beauty anyway, you might as well do so in a deliberate, self-conscious and reflective manner, rather than unconsciously and without knowing what you are doing, thereby only hitting the mark fitfully, if at all. If someday you find yourself working and operating within this reflection, you have become a Platonist.

A more difficult doctrine follows when Diotima tells Socrates that the purpose of love is to mount from beautiful objects to the source of beauty *beyond* all objects. We should ascend from single sensible beauties, or 'beauties of earth', to 'beauty absolute, separate, simple and everlasting which without diminution and without increase, or any change, is imparted to the ever-growing and perishing beauties of all other things.' If we are able to hold commerce with 'true beauty simple and divine', then we can bring forth, not images only, but realities. 'We thereby become the friend of God and immortal, in so far as man may.' (211e–212a, Jowett tr.) This source is more real, more powerful, more beautiful than any of its effects, so whatever attraction we feel for the latter, we should feel more strongly for the former. This proposal tests our belief in forms or archetypes; do they really exist? If so, where? And how can you admire the beauty of something you cannot see?

Aristotle apparently failed this test. For this student of Plato the forms are real, but not separate from the objects they characterize. He retained Plato's speculation on one point, however; this naturalist conceded that there is *one* object that is as unchanging as Parmenides and Plato claimed the forms are and thus not part of our world of change. This thing moves all other objects by attraction, itself unmoved. It is the final cause of the universe, but it cannot be the efficient cause because it must be engaged in the highest activity, directed towards the highest object. It can only be described as thought thinking itself. It cannot know us, because knowledge brings about a union between knower and object known. If it were to know us, it would immediately fall to our level, into motion, and cease to be perfect. Aristotle cannot explain why there is a cosmos; strictly speaking, there should only be the absolute separate substance knowing itself. It is a 'black hole' that absorbs all energy into itself, allowing none to escape. Aristotle waved away this problem: the universe is eternal and thus does not need a first cause—but this is to confuse temporal origin with philosophical dependence. In his own language, all moving substances confess themselves to be dependent; none fully explains itself nor can explain the rest of the cosmos.

Plotinus was a Greek-speaking Egyptian who was born near Alexandria around 200 CE and later migrated to Rome. He addressed this problem by going back to Plato and enlarging on the ways Plato had rebelled against the Parmenidean convention that true being must be unchanging. His point of departure was Plato's highest form, the Good. The 'Good' for Plato is naturally self-diffusive; that is, it spontaneously spreads or communicates itself. Secondly, Plato described this highest form as 'beyond Being', that is, beyond the unchanging rigidity of the forms. Both claims open up the possibility of a dynamism in the highest principle. Plotinus concentrated on Plato's Pythagorean tradition from the *Timaeus* of the generation of the cosmos from a mathematical monad and a complementary dyadic principle. Building on this insight Plotinus went one better than Plato, soaring into transcendence by postulating an ultimate simple whose radical otherness lifted it above the stability necessary for human knowledge, but also freed it to express the goodness whose explosion explained the world. This is the 'One', a negative term that means without division or parts of any kind. This tells us what it is not and that we cannot know it, for our knowledge is based on structure, and this principle has no structure. It cannot have any other name, because every name highlights one trait at the expense of opposites; but this principle excludes nothing and accounts for everything.

The difficulty of generating multiplicity from unity has attracted considerable interest. Plotinus says the One '"overflows" and its excess begets an other than itself.' (V.2.1, O'Brien tr.) Overflowing is an analogy with a liquid and conveys the inexhaustible richness of the One, but it exists in some tension with the equally firm statement that the One is self-complete and needs nothing—in particular, it does not need to produce anything beyond itself. Overflowing also suggests loss of control or a mistake. Plotinus explains more fully later: 'In turning toward itself the One sees. It is this seeing that constitutes the Intelligence.' (V. 1. 7) That is, the One's seeing itself produces a second principle of Intelligence as a side-effect. Later Neoplatonists will seize on this device to explain the production of further and lower emanations. Specifically, each principle or hypostasis contemplates, but it may contemplate what is above it, in which case it rises to its proper level, fulfillment and perfection, or it may contemplate itself, in which case it gives rise to a level below itself. In general, all hypostases are called to imitate the One and thus rise to union with it as far as they can. The one way they should *not* imitate the highest principle is to pretend they *are* the One, or pretend that self-contemplation is their proper and highest activity. To use later language, they may understand themselves through their *cause*, in which case they rise *toward* their cause; or they may know themselves through *themselves*, in which case they give rise to a lower level, towards which they try to imitate the One again by acting as lord or ruler. According to Plotinus, lower soul falls into the matter it is trying to govern, becoming embodied, divided and affected by what it is attempting to shape and subdue. Such effort is tragically unnecessary, since higher soul, which does not fall, orders matter as far as this is possible by simply contemplating what is above itself. It is this rebellion or apostasy by lower soul, this attempt to eclipse or usurp the place of the One, that creates the lower reaches and specious drama of the cosmos, until lower soul realizes its error, the futility of its disobedience, gives up its subversion, converts and re-joins higher soul. Although Plotinus formally opposed the Gnostics, this may have been because he sensed an inner affinity between their worldview and his own; that is, the production of the lower levels of the cosmos and the fall of soul into matter never should have happened, and will be reversed in an eschaton or final condition. Salvation consists in escape, in rolling back creation, for the world of matter is inherently unstable and chaotic; it cannot be further redeemed.

A further benefit of age is that it allows us to see that, in spite of the arbitrary or jury-rigged character of his theory of 'emanation', there is a good deal of practical wisdom concentrated in Plotinus' intellectual scheme. The lower circles are darker, less real, characterized by division, compulsion and frenetic motion. The circle in which you find yourself fixes most aspects of your existence, including your psychological, ethical, even economic or professional life; it determines what you find interesting and what you think is irrelevant. In other words, once you are in a circle, much about your life becomes inevitable. The spectrum of options before you are all you take to exist; your choices become almost predetermined. The formula for happiness consists in discovering which circle you belong in, and reaching it. Testing different lifestyles, different professions—even different possible marriage partners—is largely a question of deciding what circle you could find happiness in. Most of us eventually get at least close to our true circle, for over time life has a way of grading our potential, of educating our ambitions, schooling our motives, letting us know what we can be, down to the third decimal point. This can be a painful, even a brutal process. Life disabuses us of our illusions, it winnows and sifts our presumptions. If we persevere, however, if we are open and honest, it eventually acquaints us with a realm where we feel at home, can do something interesting, of which we can even be proud. Our idealism is naïve and needs to be tempered. The world is not a uniformly good place, so we make adjustments.

When we are growing up, any figure from a higher circle appears as a 'savior'. He doesn't have to come from the highest principle, from the 'One'; any circle above us will do. His effect can be electric. He seems to descend from some superior place, not bothered by the divisions, compulsions or frenzy of the world we inhabit. In contrast, he seems 'cool', relaxed, detached. 'Salvation' for us then consists in pulling ourselves up to where such people exist. If we look back to the influence of our parents, of the teachers and mentors who have helped us, this is in fact what they did. We get different things from different people, of course; one person doesn't have to give us everything, or be good across the board before we accept some good thing from them. We overlook or sidestep deficiencies in our mentors to take advantage of the one area where they can make a real difference for us. As we look back over our formation, it can seem as though we 'swung' from one mentor to the next—if we were lucky. If you were fortunate enough to have had a first, you sometimes must wait a good while for the next. Sometimes we have to imagine the mentor, the 'savior' from above, to get the effect; it's surprising that this works almost as well. In the process of maturing, we are all at least partially autodidacts, because we are all somewhat inadequately parented. Yet salvation in this sense is not rare, for as young people we are amazingly resilient and resourceful.

Art is a first 'salvation'. Making something beautiful, something you enjoy experiencing just to experience it, not for any particular purpose or outside value—is to escape the tyranny of time and pull yourself to a higher level that is less divided, less compulsory and less frenetic than our everyday world. Art provides access to form or archetype, it allows for a greater order, predictability and calm than is normally available, yet can also present a window back on the work-a-day world from which it departs and which it may depict, opening the possibility of insight and wonder. Art allows a greater focus, concentration and power in my experience because form brings a discipline and economy towards a single effect which invests the work with a richness of content, a cargo of awareness and memories and an intensity that exceeds everyday experience. 'A thing of beauty is a joy forever', as Keats tells us. Art is a first victory over death. Great art is immortal, and makes us aware, perhaps for the first time, of immortality, of things that don't age or change. The beautiful interrupts and provides a release from time while we enjoy it, it reconciles the polarities and divisions that battle one another in our lives and which at the practical level can leave us exhausted and bitter. Form gives us the superiority of insight, it allows art to allay our fears and calm our anxieties; it establishes a separating distance and protective detachment against terror, against the sublime, similar to the 'sacred canopy' that religion provides against the evil of the world which it similarly allows us to contemplate safely, and then returns us to our ordinary lives carrying a bit of higher motivation and more noble nature into our encounter with these same forces which we now know better. Art offers an intimation and foretaste that there is something higher than what we ordinarily experience. Production of art offers salvation in another way, because working on art, something that is planned from a beginning towards a goal, that has preparation, scope and order, means that one day this work will come to an end. Like God, we will rest on the seventh day. This is a luxury, and already the mark of a higher Plotinian circle, a noble or aristocratic existence; for without form, our work goes on forever.

Even work is a kind of salvation—again because of form. For all our complaints about it, it's no secret that many people find weekends and holidays more difficult to negotiate, principally because they haven't found a satisfying way of spending their leisure time. Without the discipline and routine of work we are forced to confront time without our everyday weapon—our job. Work fixes this dilemma; we don't have to plan much; it's taken care of ahead of time. Specialists in psychological interrogation tell us that unstructured time is one of the most difficult experiences for humans to endure. The first thing you do when interrogating a terror suspect is to take away all the clocks and watches, tape the windows to remove any indication of day or night, so that time becomes an unmanageable psychological weight and finally a torture. From many perspectives, time is our enemy, even though we swim in time as a fish swims in the sea. For the Greeks, motion was a sign of imperfection, and for Aristotle time is the measure of motion. St. Paul tells us we are here to 'redeem' the time; form is unquestionably the instrument by which we achieve our most interesting, impressive and satisfying redemptions, although we never fully overcome time. Rather, we harness it, shape it and make it serve our own purposes.

In book IV of John Milton's *Paradise Lost*, Satan describes his experience of being cast out of heaven:

> Me miserable! Which way shall I flee
> Infinite wrath, and infinite despair?
> Which way I flee is Hell, my self am Hell,
> And in the lowest deep a lower deep
> Still threatening to devour me opens wide,
> To which the Hell I suffer seems a Heav'n (73–78).

Satan inhabits Plotinian space, circles upon circles descending from the pin-prick of white light down to the lowest shade of matter. Space is not homogeneous or only quantitatively differentiated; it is not Newtonian; rather, it is qualitatively differentiated. Satan falls *down* and *out*; each lower circle is darker than the one above, there is a corresponding loss of coherence and contemplation, an increase of division, compulsion and motion, a growing sense of frustration and futility. Thus in a sense even Satan finds his proper circle, for though damned he is immortal. He has rejected Christ as God's favorite, and he plots henceforth to undermine the mission Christ has accepted, the salvation of the human race.

Because of Milton's opposition to the monarchy during the English civil war, he gives a sympathetic depiction to Lucifer who is in similar revolt against a monarchic God. As William Blake put it, Milton was 'a true poet and of the devil's party without knowing it'; that is, Lucifer is the real hero of *Paradise Lost*. Milton makes a further change to the traditional story; he heightens Satan's rebellion. As Harold Bloom writes, 'Satan, until the nasty surprise of learning that he owes his very existence to Christ, had been the glorious Lucifer, foremost among God's loyal flatterers. Down he comes, upon ceasing to be his father's favourite, and as he starts downward and outward he declares that he has fathered himself.'1 As Satan says in Book Five:

> 'That we were formd then saist thou? & the work
> Of secondarie hands, by task transferd
> From Father to his Son? strange point and new!
> Doctrin which we would know whence learnt: who saw
> When this creation was? rememberst thou
> Thy making, while the Maker gave thee being?
> We know no time when we were not as now;
> Know none before us, self-begot, self-rais'd
> By our own quick'ning power, when fatal course
> Had circl'd his full Orbe, the birth mature
> Of this our native Heav'n, Ethereal Sons.
> Our puissance is our own, our own right hand
> Shall teach us highest deeds, by proof to try
> Who is our equal' Bk. 5, 854–866.

Not only does Lucifer dispute with Christ the premier spot in creation, he goes further to deny that God is his creator. He is 'self-begot'. This breathtaking statement is unprecedented in the western canon. Never before in the tradition has an author placed such a statement in the mouth of a creature. Had an author a hundred years before Milton attempted such a thing, he would have been burned at the stake, by both Protestants and Catholics alike. Milton gets away with it by placing it in the mouth of a devil, thus distancing himself from it while simultaneously introducing its provocative and disturbing claim.

This boast by such an intelligent creature stuns the mind and beggars the imagination. Has Colleridge's 'willing suspension of disbelief', necessary for all fiction, been stretched here so far that it begins to tear? Has Milton gone too far? Is he making too great a demand upon his readership? On the face of it it seems a mistake, an imprudent as well as impious move. In advancing from perceived injustice to ontological implausibility, has Milton made a poetic blunder, undercutting the respect and sympathy he seeks to generate for his hero? Has Satan damaged his case by giving way to emotional spleen, leading him to an intemperate and regrettable excess? Does this risk pushing his pose of solemn indignation and sense of injured merit into a ridiculous pomposity and strained over-reaction? Has adult resistance and impressive courage collapsed into childish stubbornness, juvenile backlash and the spiteful resort to a maximal response with a blasphemy beyond all blasphemies, whose intended threat and desire to hurt are undercut by its obvious lack of foundation?

Or does this heightening rather enhance the power of the poem? Does it allow Milton to portray one possible response to the slight and extraordinary demand God is making on his highest creature? According to Aristotle, in constructing a plot it is preferable to choose a plausible impossibility over an implausible possibility (*Poetics*, Bk. 7). Does this gambit by Milton jog our imaginations to recognize a not unfamiliar behavior that upset and frustrated expectations may lead to? By its very over-the-top-ness, does this change rather increase the power of the story exponentially by moving the depiction closer to an all-too-human reaction? Milton's heightening may then be false to the traditional story but psychologically and artistically true. For an artist is an oracle; he says some things whether he means to say them or not, even whether they support his brief or not. We leave our fingerprint in everything we do and give ourselves away to a trained eye even in our most brilliant stratagems and deceits. The rejection of the father, the *denial* of the father *as* the father, is a new turn that is prescient and prophetic for the future.

Milton's Lucifer became the archetype and inspiration for the Romantic poets who similarly feel themselves thrown down and out, slipping and sliding in a circle of error, squalor and weakness, charged with creating beauty from unworthy materials with inadequate tools—with making bricks without straw by an unfair or perhaps absent paternity. They seized on the sympathetic depiction of Lucifer by Milton for their distinctive theory of the artistic 'genius'. The depiction of the artist as a genius consists in a 'secularization' of Milton's Lucifer, that is, the transfer of this central claim by Lucifer from the angelic realm to the human realm. The Romantic artist rejects the classical vocation of art as *mimesis*.

Mimesis is a Greek word meaning to imitate or to copy. Until the 19th century it was maintained that all art is mimetic, that is, it consists of an imitation of reality, either of a Platonic form in its ideal, or of an individual in its singularity. The artist-as-genius rejects this vocation, he is in no sense 'mimetic'. On the contrary, he claims to be literally *creative*—he brings something into being that did not exist before. This means, however, that he is usurping the role of God; he solves the problem of the inadequate Father by denying the Father, whose 'reality' is not worth imitating. Further divine-like traits are added as this theory develops from Kant to Schopenhauer. Unlike ordinary mortals, and especially his 'bourgeois' audience, the artist-as-genius is determined not by 'horizontal' forces streaming upon him from the 'phenomenal' world; he has attenuated their power by severing his links with the world of fashionable patronage, overthrowing his 'anxiety of influence' before the masterpieces of the past and the tyranny of conventional taste. By cutting such links he claims to have reached 'vertical determination', making contact with the hidden 'noumenal' core beyond the realm of cause and effect, transforming himself into an oracle by which this hidden divinity—his true self—may speak a 'new word' and bestow value upon an otherwise flat world of unworthy motives.

What is serious about this is that in the modern period the artist-as-genius becomes the archetype for human fulfillment and perfection: we should *all* be 'geniuses'; this is as high as human beings can reach. The artist as genius jumps before the saint of the Middle Ages and the scientist of the Enlightenment as a model to be imitated, and this archetype is based on Milton's Lucifer. This reaction—involving a 'killing' or wiping away of the Father—is the radical modern solution to the problem of the inadequate father.

If we turn by contrast to the Christian scriptures, what disturbed the Pharisees about Jesus was his warm intimacy with the God of the Temple and Law, an unbecoming and perhaps presumptuous familiarity towards the object of sacrifice who is properly treated as somewhat distant and fearsome. Where did he get this? Where did it come from? Can such an attitude be correct? This question is similar to the one we asked apropos of Diotima's speculation that the source of beauty must itself be beautiful, in fact more beautiful than its effects: how could she know this? Why must it be more beautiful? Jesus goes out of his way to stress that he is not 'self-begot'; on the contrary, he traces his origin repeatedly and daringly to the 'heavenly Father'. To the charge that he is innovating, he continually downplays his originality or creativity, stressing instead his subordination and obedience. If he changes the tradition, it is because he speaks with the authority of the 'Father'; where he is original, it is because he sees the 'new thing' the Father is doing. This speculative intimacy lay behind his ministry; the power seemed to flash out of him. Jesus didn't just quote scripture, saying you could interpret it this way or interpret it that way; he corrected scripture, in fact, he made new scripture. Where did such a power come from? Joseph, his natural father, had died. Was this perhaps some form of compensation reaction? No one can see God, so how did Jesus know his 'Father' was like this? For that matter, how did he know God *was* his father, who cared about him, who had a project for him? And turning it around, wasn't this request unfair? Why can't the Father do these things himself, or have done them long before Jesus ever appeared? Why does he *need* Jesus at all? One thinks of the scene in the Garden of Gethsemane—Jesus asking that the cup be passed from him, but that nonetheless he will carry out the Father's will. It was all so unnecessary and cruel. And further, if the Father *can't* do it, if he *hasn't* done it, how is the *Son* supposed to do it? Where is the Son supposed to get the *power* to do it? You can't get blood from a stone, as they say, and the apple doesn't fall far from the tree. There may be something fishy, suspect or unacceptable about this plot, despite its familiarity. We can sum up this objection by saying that actuality cannot exceed potentiality.

It cannot, and yet in our experience such requests are made routinely, and routinely accepted, even routinely carried out. Such a request could even be said to *constitute* the relation between father and son in our earthly condition and in our everyday experience. Father and son are in one sense distinct, but in another sense they are one. So, in that sense, the father *is* carrying out the deed; he is carrying out the deed *through* his son. All the son's power does indeed come from the father; he has nothing separate by which he could be carrying it out. So everything is in order.

Jesus couldn't see his heavenly father; like Diotima, he was engaged in speculation. Like all human sons, he worked with an archetype.2 This is where he got his new power. He found a *new* father, of whom the first was only an anticipation, a precursor, a foreshadowing, a suggestion. He had to be able to discern the form through the particular; more accurately, he had to see the particular *as* a limited copy of the archetype it could not fully express. This is not unusual; in fact, it's a practice we all engage in, repeatedly, all the time; it is one we must engage in if we are to move forward through life's novel dilemmas. All our power does indeed come from a father; we are carrying out a mission, something a father has given us or would at least approve of, something which, for whatever reason, he could not achieve himself. But then in a sense he *is* achieving it—through us. While commonplace, this practice is noteworthy, and has a significant alternative. Ultimately, we resolve the dilemma of the absent, outrageous or inadequate father either the way Lucifer did or the way Jesus did. The point is that the way Jesus did, far from being atypical, idiosyncratic or bizarre, is common, routine and normative—in fact, definitory for our species, although beginning with Milton it is challenged more and more by the alternative.

This means that our initial perception was not correct. Actuality does not exceed potentiality, for there *was* more potential in the situation than we suspected. It *is* possible to get blood from a stone—if you are a Platonist. We see the archetype *in* the particular, and act on this basis. Both as a civilization and as individuals, we regularly and routinely *do* pull ourselves up by our own bootstraps.

What kind of story do we have to tell ourselves for this miracle to happen? For some reason the father was indisposed, preoccupied or otherwise engaged. But the task seems so unfair, the mission so difficult, perhaps something deeper was involved—a radical insurrection, an earlier fundamental rejection: the freedom of creatures who rebelled, bringing an unhinged quality to the universe that could only be resolved by a reverse act of free creation. For Plotinus, this was the option by lower soul to contemplate itself, to imitate the One in the way not permitted, by pretending to actually *be* the One; similarly with Milton, this unhinged quality was for Lucifer to reject not only Christ as his rival, but the Father as his creator. The Father could not correct this situation by divine *Fiat*; this would not respect creaturely freedom; it would not heal the wound that needed to be healed. The Father delegates the Son, and the Son accepts the mission under obedience. The concept of 'son' both distinguishes and connects. The Son accepts that the Father wanted to do this, *would* have done it if he could, but for some reason had to renege, default or pass it on—because he *is* the Father. The Father *is* doing it in the only way he can –*through* the Son—for at a deeper level the Father and Son are one.

The Son shows his acceptance of the Father by calling him 'abba', instead of distancing himself from him or becoming angry with him. One cannot imagine Lucifer calling the Father 'abba'. With Jesus *this* is where the exchange and commingling of power occurs. He accepts and uses the power he receives from the Father. In his mind, he is acting as the Father's delegate or viceroy, the 'face' of the Father in this new situation. The Son's conviction is that the Father, while declining the job himself, has not absconded. He has not left the Son bereft or with inadequate resources. It comes down to the fact that Jesus must choose between an identity as Son or some other identity. The ultimate question for him, as for us, is 'Who are you?' By offering his support and power, by declaring him 'Son', the Father comes as close to Jesus as possible, without *imposing* an identity or taking away his freedom. For Jesus the resulting oneness explains his power; his mission is to defend the Father's identity and fidelity to a doubting generation. For the bystanders all that he says is speculative, when not vaguely blasphemous or threatening to strict monotheism. At Caesarea Philippi, the apostle Peter comes to see what Jesus sees; he comes to perceive the Father *through* the deeds of the Son. He sees the form or archetype *through* the particular.

If the Trinity is active in creation, then we should expect to find traces of the Trinity in creation. We do indeed find traces of the Trinity everywhere—this is one of the 'voices' that as we get older the stones themselves begin to speak. Specifically, we find a trace of the Trinity in every father-son relationship.3 With the obediential response that Jesus performs, the son *becomes* the more adequate father, or the adequate expression of a father who has become questionable to his world, thanks to which the father-figure is restored to his former position of respect, admiration and power, to which the world can again respond with love and fecundity. Life is (again) worth living, and is worth repeating. It makes sense to bring new people into the world, because they will find it an agreeable and satisfying place to live, and later to bring forth their own children as well. This need never have happened. It is one of the defined conciliar doctrines that Jesus' human will remained free even of his divine

The Sorrow That Dares Not Say Its Name; The Inadequate Father, the Motor of History

will. In the metaphysical relationship, however, the son's role is crucial for the father—for him to continue to *act* and *function* as Father. The Son's role as savior is an extension and completion of the Father's work as creator, not a desperate 'plan B' suddenly added on when creation went suddenly and unexpectedly awry. Rather, the Son's role as savior is essential if the Father is to continue to function effectively as creator. This is the pulse-beat of history, the Son completing, and thereby restoring the credibility of the Father, in a continuous feed-back mechanism, the former supporting the latter, the latter completing the former, in a relationship that is ultimately one of absolute mutual trust and devotion which is not mysterious because, as said, at this level Father and Son are one. It is one mission that defines them both, in a world that has been given over to freedom.

Dostoevsky clearly believes that, in *The Brothers Karamosov,* the father drove his sons to their murder, and that in a sense it is a communal act. Like Lucifer, they have sought to deny or erase their inadequate father. Only Alyosha is insulated by his option for religion from this; only he escapes the contaminating poison. The others are sinned against, but carry on in various ways the evil they have inherited, harming all who come close, including one another.

Alyosha has fashioned a new image of the father; one could say that, in his religious vocation, he has passed himself along to a 'different' father he could glimpse only minimally, obliquely and with great difficulty in his birth father. This idealized Father is limited by human freedom and its trajectory in history; that is, he is not able to set all right or do all he might have wanted. In particular, he cannot make the birth father all he should have been—and Alyosha must accept this. But with his new archetype, this is not a difficulty; Alyosha has shrugged, said 'OK', and moved on. How different for his brothers, who cannot come either to accept or to finally break with the father they have inherited. They are still 'one' with this father at an unconscious level and in spite of their hatred for him. One could say that Alyosha has extracted himself and gone forward in a situation where his brothers, who were in a sense more 'objective' or 'realistic', remained stuck and controlled by their initial condition. In one sense, he was the impractical one, the idealistic and other-worldly 'dreamer'. But ultimately who is more shrewd or clever in his response to their common situation?

Alyosha was fortunate in that this alternative archetype was supplied by his religion—in Christianity's depiction of the Father's extraordinary request and the Son's equally extraordinary response. Without Alyosha's solution, his brothers' fate is sealed; they cannot escape the burden they have inherited; they have no alternative but to carry on and return in kind the paternal tendencies they detested.

Christ and Lucifer are also brothers. They are born of the same Father, both the acme of creation, both the apple of the Father's eye. They serve as archetypes in that they indicate two ways of responding to the perceived inadequacy in the father, the request to go beyond the father, to accept an unfair situation and difficult mission that involves humiliation and possible failure to do something the father, if he is truly 'all-powerful', arguably could have or should have taken care of beforehand. Archetypes are more than convenient fictions, lazy stereotypes or false generalizations that take the place of real thinking. They are richer, more powerful and more productive than the flat analytical concepts which as we age we gradually slough off. Both Lucifer and Jesus have a rationale behind them, a species of justification to defend their opposed interpretations and responses. The situation is conflicted, but not underdetermined. Lucifer's response is still a rebellion, a violent alteration, ultimately re-configuring the situation with himself as self-fathered or self-begot. Jesus's response carries on the received vocabulary where he accepts the Father as father. Jesus's option is difficult, but not for that reason unnatural or unprecedented; rather it is almost routine or normative for the species. Rather than wiping away the Father in a daring usurpation, Jesus remains continuous with and faithful to an identity as Son by defending and then demonstrating the Father's creative, covenantal fidelity. Although ultimate in the sense of unsurpassable, his response falls in line with a series of such archetypal responses in evolutionary history without which there would have been no progress or indeed survival.4 At the end of Plato's *Symposium*, when Alcibiades makes his comic entrance, wine has loosened his tongue and he says that although Socrates is physically unattractive, 'Once I caught him when he was open like Silenus' statues, and I had a glimpse of the figures he keeps hidden within: they are so godlike—so bright and beautiful, so utterly amazing—that I no longer had a choice. I just had to do whatever he told me.' (216e–

217a). Without the alternative archetype now available through the gospel, we would be condemned to the same behaviour as Dimitri, Ivan and Smerdyakov in the conflicted, unfair—or worse—situations in which we sometimes find ourselves. So close are these two fraternal archetypes that in Jerome's Latin translation of the Bible, the term 'Lucifer' refers to Christ, not to Satan. In Ps. 110.3 and in 2 Peter 1:19 it is used for Venus, the morning star that announces the dawn, which also refers to Christ. With the death and resurrection of Jesus, each morning heralds a new day, potentially unlike the day before.

Notes

[1] *Ruin the Sacred Truths*: *Poetry and Belief from the Bible to the Present*, Harvard UP, 1991, p. 112.

[2] On the vexed question of Jesus' sense of his vocation and consciousness of his identity, Nicholas Perrin builds a powerful case that Jesus was the founder of one of several counter-temple movements during the first century of the common era. These movements were united by the common conviction that the debased, venal and illegitimate high priestly elite had rendered ritually impure the Jerusalem temple (and indeed the entire land) and thereby inaugurated the 'tribulations' and 'time of woes' that would precede and accompany God's definitive intervention and the installation of the eschatological temple 'not made with human hands'. These movements used apocalyptic texts like Isaiah 56, Jeremiah 7, and Zechariah 14 as 'lenses' through which to view their own time and as 'scripts' by which their own history was being structured. It was in these texts that they looked to discover their roles in this final drama. Since only the eschatological high priest could establish the definitive, final temple, Jesus interpreted this role—by default—as his own. In other words, the corporate history of Israel came first and was paramount in every Jew's mind; individual roles came second, and were derivative from the former. Perrin writes: '... (L)ike John the Baptizer before him and the early Church after him, Jesus found the temple of his day to be corrupt, inferred from this—as did his cousin John— the onset of messianic tribulation, and then finally saw his own calling as a response to this divinely ordained crisis' p. 78. Here Jesus also functions as a model or archetype for his followers: 'Like these other counter-temple

sectarians, the Christians interpreted their own suffering as part and parcel of their priestly calling. If suffering was the overture to the final drama, then the heroes were to play out their roles until the curtain should close again to the applause of heaven. The curtain would not come to a close apart from their fulfilling the terms of their assigned script.' P. 77 See Nicholas Perrin, *Jesus the Temple*, Grand Rapids/London, Baker Academic, 2010.

[3] Hans Urs von Balthasar discusses the Trinity as an archetype for comprehending the parent-child relationship in *Theo-Logic, vol. II, Truth of God*, tr. Adrian J. Walker, San Francisco, Ignatius Press, 2004, p. 59. He finds that the love of two people coming together to create a third 'remains, in spite of all the obvious dissimilarities, the most eloquent *imago Trinitatis* that we find woven into the fabric of the creature' (p. 62).

[4] This appreciation of Christ as an 'archetype' for our consideration and imitation is similar to the appreciation von Balthasar develops of the 'normative archetypal quality' that attends the role Jesus takes on in the 'theo-drama' of world history. He writes: 'In the role of God, Jesus Christ is his valid exposition and presence in the world' but at the same time 'the role played by Jesus Christ yields the principle for allotting roles to all the other actors', and so 'it is from this center that human conscious subjects are allotted personalizing roles or missions (charisms)'. *Theo-Drama: Theological Dramatic Theory*, vol. III, *Dramatis Personae: Persons in Christ*, tr. Graham Harrison, San Francisco, Ignatius Press, 1992, pp. 257–8.

CHAPTER 7

CHRISTIANITY AND THE DEATH PENALTY

What should be the Christian attitude towards the death penalty? The Church has never ruled it out as immoral. However, contemporary Liberalism tends to view it as the barbaric vestige of an unenlightened age, and many Christians esteem that Christianity should be at least as compassionate as Liberalism. This is contested, however, because Christianity has never considered life in this world as the highest value. As self-seeking narcissism becomes the accepted default ethic of our time, however, the one place Liberalism seems to concede that the death penalty may be permitted and even necessary is when narcissism grows beyond civilized bounds and tolerates murder as a violation of the earlier 'human right' to life, unapologetically viewing other people reductively as either instruments for or obstacles to a subject's personal advancement. When they develop into the latter, they may conveniently but unobtrusively be gotten 'out of the way'.

The moral propriety of imposing the death penalty continues to bedevil Christian discussions of responsible and enlightened judicial practice in an era characterized by both a psychologically inflected and more compassionate understanding of human agency on the one hand and unprecedented, flamboyant crimes of human cruelty, torture and death - as in anonymous serial killing - on the other. The psychological pressure that the Christian position on capital punishment should, for that reason, be different from a 'secular' viewpoint, interpreted as unavoidably cruel because an immediate deliverance from 'natural' or 'unconverted' impulses towards retaliation or 'pay-back', sets up expectations that influence the discussion in certain *fora*, as it does occasionally its opposite—the expectation that Christianity must treat all people equally. and without embarrassment call all to live up to similar basic standards of propriety and morality. Early Christian communities impressed their neighbors by the fact that (1) they were made up of members from different ethnic groups and social backgrounds, and (2) they were careful not to become a social nuisance, draw attention to themselves or burden the larger population, by taking care of their own through mutual aid and charity. When Christianity became the official cult of the empire, sooner or later it had to address the death sentence.

Christian authors never ruled out the death penalty as inherently immoral. It was retained as an acceptable penalty for the most serious offenses—murder, treason, banditry, insurrection, mutiny, etc. That the state had to be ruled by an authority, disobedience to whom in important matters was appropriately punished by death, was widely accepted and practiced. In an era where each city had its 'official' divine patron, devotion to 'strange' gods coming from distant parts of the empire (or beyond) were carefully monitored as possible covers for rebellion or provocations towards social disturbance. All the Christian apostles we know of - including St. Paul - were put to death.

Jesus never prayed in the temple. He *taught* in the temple. When he wanted to pray, he withdrew to a deserted place and spent the night alone. Further, he had the habit of referring to the Jewish God as 'my Father'—a scandalously presumptuous, deliberately provocative and astronomically self-centering utterance for a Jewish male to make. When John the Baptist was executed for criticizing the marriage of his Roman governor, Jesus seems to have gotten the message concerning the fate his disruptive social behavior might be leading him towards; he henceforth turned aside political or military inquiries. Also, his riding into Jerusalem on a prophetic donkey, rather than a Davidic stallion—as also his punishing the money-changers carrying out legitimate business in the forecourt of the Temple—were clear evidence that he had narrowed and specified - rather than completely abandoned - his fate. He would expend himself - in fact, give his life - for the 'restoration of the Kingdom of Israel', but the latter would take a form different from the independent, self-standing monarchy his rivals in the rebellion after his death dreamed of. The ancient ambition of Israel to become a 'great kingdom' towards which all the nations of the earth would come streaming' died a horrific and exorbitantly cruel death, involving a humiliation and misery that became legendary. They did indeed become a dire warning and forbidding example to the wider world, but not in the manner in which they first imagined themselves.

Death was not final for Jesus, and death is not final for a Christian. After death there is judgment. Judgment is related to what we inherited and to what we leave for others—to legacy received and to legacy established for those who will come after - because the latter affected why we made certain choices. No one knows all that goes on in judgment, but it would be a mistake to take it lightly; God deals with adults, not children; all our excuses go by the board. We are not responsible for everything that happened, but we are responsible for what we did. All our possibilities, all our graces, as well as all our handicaps and difficulties are taken into account. The point I wish to make here is the unique dignity that characterizes this occasion and its proceedings. Our basic choices are set in sharp relief. Mitigating circumstances wash away as blurring the main point. Mood and season of the original act are airbrushed aside. Historical accidents that accompanied or attended a decision made years before 'melt' backwards; leaving only the 'headline'. Nor is each thing final, for its significance changes and depends on what we built upon it later. One reason we value sports records as unique is that they seem fixed and unchanging - almost the only thing that is. Yet even for these, what they 'mean' changes. Indeed, for everything we do, what they 'mean' changes with each passing moment, as its historical legacy spills further outward. For example, why compete in sports at all? Thus in the end, we are responsible - as responsible as we allow ourselves to become.

Judgment is the most serious dignity we have. Animals don't have judgment, for no one holds them responsible for what happens to them. Animals are dependent upon us for what happens to them. For better or for worse, we have taken the world upon our necks, and it is impossible to pull it off or give it back. You can't see it—we look like the other animals—but from that first moment on, we go together and cannot become unstuck. Every decision we make affects this 'world' one can't see but to which we are attached - not just our personal world, but also the 'common world' which our actions participate in, build up or tear down, rearrange, for which as a consequence we as a whole are loosely responsible. The latter functions as a kind of report card or rolling account, giving sum totals and average values on the myriad topics we think about, discuss or make a decision on. Our faces fall into pre-human inscrutability as we try to escape responsibility, but our actions betray our true feelings and give our actual positions away. Through them people can look at our personal world as at an unmade bed, and then look back at us. 'What are you doing to us?' they ask. Moving from the personal to the common world is the most serious way we have of affecting one another, by pointing out hitherto unseen dimensions that can change what things *mean*.

This is where capital punishment becomes an issue.

As said, extending an action from our personal world to the common world is a tentative attempt at establishing a *value*. The common world is always already semi-established. Although open to new suggestions, it codifies what has so far been considered valuable. The work-a-day presumption is that whatever reinforces, anchors or extends lines of value already established is itself valuable. This direction could be altered by a revolutionary experience, but after many generations the burden of proof lies on the other side. We are ourselves evaluated, and evaluate others, by how much they contribute towards, correctly appraise and successfully obtain what our common world considers valuable. Sometimes our attempts to propose a new value are beaten back as inexperienced, short-sighted or immature; other times they are tentatively accepted. As the weight of experience grows, however, the attitude of the common world towards uncommon proposals and untried initiatives becomes wary, skeptical and negative. It simply becomes harder and harder to find something truly new; also, there can be long-term consequences to an initially attractive suggestion that detract from or compromise the first impression. Most of the good things in life have already been discovered.

Discussions of taking away life as a judicial punishment—even for murder - are tricky for several reasons. First, there is the worry that a request for this punishment stems from emotion or a desire for revenge. Might we not be applying the principle of 'an eye for an eye' too literally or conveniently—simply because we don't know any better, or other possibility? Secondly, following this principle will in no way bring back the initial victim. If this punishment does nothing to restore the lost party, does not having recourse to it begin to appear both useless and barbaric? Aren't we just 'piling up bodies' to satisfy an abstract principle that does nothing to improve the situation for either side in the criminal offense? The problem here is that death is a unique condition, and killing someone even in what appears 'just' or 'equal' punishment involves entering an unfamiliar and scary zone—unlike others, it is final - where humans feel out of place because they are radically 'out of their depth'. It is like an 'oxygen-free' zone where we don't belong. Death is the arena of our 'absolute fate'; it is perhaps for God alone to make a reckoning there.

On the other hand, doing less seems equally unacceptable. Further, the gravity of the initial act seems such that the forfeit of the guilty party's life appears not unreasonable or beyond rational consideration. After all, if he took away such a unique and all-including value from another person, the forfeit of the same value on his side would not seem to be placed beyond the scope of civilized discussion or behavior. It is a limited but possible option. Although a radical value, it is still a this-worldly value. What makes it so different that we hesitate, or that the discussion about it becomes so intense?

All traditional cultures have made room for death as a possible punishment, and some have had recourse to it on a scale and with an absence of the delays, agonized contortions and opposition between theologians, philosophers, sociologists, psychologists, social workers, judicial scholars, social activists, astrologers, new-age prophets and trans-identity activists that leaves us today amazed at our predecessors' routine efficiency. This suggests the difference is not between a 'value' which one or the other of our cultures has 'found' or 'lost'; it is rather about a sea-change between modern and traditional cultures such that the former now looks back on the latter not as an earlier version of itself, but more radically as fundamentally different - as in fact some 'other planet'.

If we ask what distinguishes the modern world from the pre-modern in a way that is relevant to the issue of the death penalty, one could do worse than consider the drop in religious faith and the rise of individualism, the spread and endorsement of narcissism, as a desperate replacement and this-worldly compensation for the loss of the former and the traditional reward for a 'good life'. If there is no punishment or reward after death, our happiness in this world is all that really matters; how can we take umbrage at someone who unapologetically makes his material comfort, his financial and social success in this world his dominant objective and the chief concern of all his efforts—both those public and official as well as those hidden and clandestine? Who cares what people think about you after you are gone, if you were able to secure a pleasant and comfortable passage on this side of the 'great divide'? The early modern thinkers Spinoza and Machiavelli were able to stir up the dust and cloud the traditional vision of the theoretical sphere as well as proper behavior in the practical sphere. After them, there doesn't seem to be much to cling to but the individual and discussion on the wisest path to secure his fortune.

A strong foundation was given to narcissism in the English tradition with the publication of John Milton's *Paradise Lost* in 1667. Milton swings the reader's sympathies towards Satan by having the poem begin just *after* the failure of the angelic revolt against God and the arrival of the new devils, to their surprise, consternation and disappointment, in hell, with some thinking that the best they could now do is to give up and beg God to be accepted back. Not so, says Satan, rallying their drooping spirits, for now they should direct their rebellious, dissatisfied energies to spoiling the new tack God is taking, offering a covenant to his new creation, humankind, to replace the failed attempt and unsatisfactory outcome of that with the angelic spirits. The reader feels sorry for the despondent angels at this point, and even admires Satan for his resilient pluck and courage. He is the only one in the poem who is close to being a 'hero', and much attention is given to his psychological development and maneuvering. Not that he is constrained, as punishment for his fall, to speaking only the truth; he more than fulfills his reputation as the 'prince of lies', but this is developed in an interesting way by his later effort to defend his rebellion, to distract, confuse and seduce the loyal angel Abdiel, with a spectacular denial that God even created him! In original narcissistic fashion he declares he has created himself:

> That we were formed then saist thou? & the work
> Of secondarie hands, by task transferred
> From Father to his Son? Strange point and new!
> When this creation was? Rememberst thou
> Thy making, while the Maker gave thee being?
> We know no time when we were not as now,

> Know none before us, self-begot, self-rais'd
> By our own quick'ning power, when fatal course
> Had circl'd his full Orbe, the birth mature
> Of this our native Heav'n, Ethereal Sons.
> Our puissance is our own, our own right hand
> shall teach us highest deeds, by proof to try
> Who is our equal. Bk. 5, 854-866

So Satan needs not God - even to make him! Rather, he is 'self-begot'—and why should he not go on directing himself as if he were alone, independent of God and everyone else? The reader shivers at the insolent courage of so outrageous a proposal and metaphysical claim—the first time made in the Western tradition! A new option is now open to the reader—to follow Satan, sympathetically but clandestinely, in his rebellion. After all, if Satan did it, so might someone else. A door has been opened, and is no longer taboo. Also, one needn't advertise this.

The restored Stuart monarchy set a powerful example towards narcissism with James I's (1567-1625) relationship with George Villiers, Duke of Buckingham and Charles II's (1630-1685) relationship with John Wilmot, Second Earl of Rochester. However, those appalled by the behavior of the royals and seeking reform seemed themselves unable to resist narcissism, though coming from an opposite direction. The puritan Milton had been an anti-monarchical ideologue during the Civil War, barely escaping with his life. His poetry, and especially *Paradise Lost*, was his revenge—and a ticking time bomb—against this loss. William Blake carried on the same fight a century later at street level, and ushered in the Romantic movement. As a boy Blake spent not a single day in school; his parents recognized he was incorrigible—too independent and rambunctious to accept discipline. His manner of learning a text from his earliest years was to read a passage and then give his own spontaneous, imaginative 'translation' of what it meant for him. Originality was everything—a lone value in a dark universe - and without which everything was dead. 'I must create a system, or be enslaved by another man's. I will not reason and compare: my business is to create.' Milton and Blake were the creative seed of the Romantic movement; Lord Byron and Percy Shelley were its fulfillment and culmination. The latter died young and ignominiously, by accidental misstep before moral dissolution claimed them. Shelley was jealous of Byron's success; on a trip out to Italy he arranged to sail past the villa where Byron was staying, but his boat capsized, and Shelley drowned. His body was burned on the beach the following day. Through a scandalous affair with his half-sister Augusta that produced a child, Byron was ostracized and socially barred from returning to England. He fled east into revolutionary activity, culminating with his joining a volunteer group attempting to liberate Greece from the Turks. He died at age 36; the doctor could not say whether this was due to malaria or syphilis.

In one sense narcissism could not accept the death penalty, because at the abstract level death represents the end of its necessary dependence on and unavoidable foundation in consciousness. However, on the concrete level narcissism could provide protection against the terrors that arise from the prospect of death—the 'anguish of being extinguished', put out like a light, simply vanishing or being stepped on like an insect. There are diverse forms of narcissism—not simply the pursuit of power, wealth or political and social influence, but any 'mono-maniacal' point of view that proposes a single reality that swells and comes to include or constitute the entire universe—Capitalism, Marxism, Freudianism - also the strongly religious points of view, as well as any philosophical or psychological theory that the 'convert' thinks will explain everything. Conversion to and participation in such an 'enthusiasm' can compensate for and push to one side anxieties that arise from dangers to our personal existence, as the 'system' bathes us in the comforting warmth of its oceanic depths. Even if as a humble foot-soldier we should fall, the 'cause' itself will ultimately prevail. Against such a massive power, my paltry existence may shrink to the dimensions of a minor instrument that may either advance or impede the assured final victory of the single reality that its advocate believes is much larger—really, all there is.

Surprisingly, therefore, narcissism, as it often leads to advocacy for a particular wide-ranging ideology, may induce the individual to a personal acceptance of the death penalty, since he believes it will never affect him directly or the deeper cause with which he identifies; only his enemies will become its victims, as they unavoidably bow before its power. An example is King James I of England, who subscribed to the theory of the 'divine right' of kings, that is, the king is on the throne directly by the will and power of God, not indirectly through the consent or endorsement by his people. Apart from its truth or falsity, James' strenuous advocacy, his embrace and implementation of this theory (together with its allowance of the death penalty) protected him psychologically before any anxieties he might have harbored that one day he might fall victim to the latter himself (as happened to King Louis XVI of France during the Revolution).

A further example is offered by the final days of the Marxist political activist Che Guevara. Che was a revolutionary guerrilla fighter all over Latin America and in Cuba under Fidel Castro. In 1967 he was captured in Bolivia by a military patrol and told he would be executed the following day. Interestingly, this information did not cause Che to fall into deep mourning or despair as others might have. He had faith in the continued progress and ultimate victory of the Revolution. The announcement did not upset or spoil his revolutionary conviction and steadiness. He was not reduced to hysterics or to crushing psychological paralysis, as might have befallen others. The news seems only to have caused mild irritation rather than plunging him into a 'slough of despond.' He lamented his death in the sense that his absence would mean that it would take the Revolution a few extra days to be achieved. However, he was confident of its final victory, and this provided a consolation that cushioned and relativized the personal loss most of us would have taken more seriously and felt more acutely. It reconciled him to accept his imminent personal extinction.

Unfortunately, in a skeptical, unbelieving age like our own, few individuals have found an ideology sufficiently powerful, attractive or all-embracing enough to lead them to risk death for its further propagation and ultimate victory. They are consequently bereft of the ideological consolation to which James I and Che obtained access. They do not subscribe to a liberal theory of universal 'human rights.' They consistently if reductively operate on the assumption of the universal power of narcissistic self-seeking like their own. At the point where your narcissism bumps up against mine, there is only the question of who wins, and who loses. That is, at the point where the other's independent self-seeking begins to pose a boundary or limitation to my own victory, dominance or expansion, I reserve the right to treat him exclusively as the rival, obstacle or impediment he has become to my desires and ambitions, my unlimited self-expansion, and to re-deploy or re-vitalize the death penalty so as to remove him by any means possible. We are all only specimens of narcissism, strong or weak, victorious or not. At the point where your narcissism interferes with mine, social reality is reduced to a Hobbesian 'war of all against all' - which is what it has been all along. We ask for no deeper conversion than to re-define 'justice' as the supremacy of brute force, and to let the latter continue to decide the on-going contest.

CHAPTER 8

THE SUPREMACY OF GOD AND THE LOVE WITHIN GOD

The core of Christian theology can be expressed as a tension between two theological intuitions: God's supremacy, and his (contrary, but appropriate) love for his 'image' in Christ, and beyond him, in those humans who 'convert' and model themselves upon him.

God is clearly supreme, but there is a 'love' within God that is not apparent at the outset, which means that, rather than being 'upright' and dominant, he is 'concave' and pregnant with an offspring that he loves for all eternity, the adequate expression or 'image' of himself that he loves supremely because he loves himself supremely, and who is the agency of, first, the creation of creatures sufficiently gifted with intellect and freedom to receive the imprint and respond to the offer of relationship with their ultimate source, and, secondly, to expend himself in an eventual but necessary (or eventually necessary) act of self-sacrifice and rescue that produces an even more spectacular, unexpected - almost contrary-to-his nature - expression and demonstration of the goodness out of which he creates the world in the first place. The intensity of the goodness that is God and out of which he operates could not have been adequately guessed or accurately estimated apart from the demonstrations of it in creation and redemption. With these consequences of it and evidence for it lying now all about us, we are without excuse. The 'ball is now in our court', so to speak.

The conceptual difficulty of accepting—or even formulating - Christian doctrine at its inception came from its novel proclamation and subsequently central claim that the divine suffered. If you say it enough times, this becomes familiar, but such does not take away its conceptual difficulties for its first audience. In the ancient world, gods don't suffer. You will go a long way in the stories and doctrines of the ancient world before you find a god who suffers. The one exception is Dionysius, the fertility god, who each year is born in the spring, grows over the summer, matures in the autumn and dies with the chills of winter—to be born again the following spring. This is his appointed task, and he approaches eternity by carrying it out effectively without fail, year after year. Like all the gods, he imitates eternity as best he can. Gods rule, gods triumph, gods are lords—but gods do not suffer—that is not the conceptual task they are entrusted with nor the narrative 'work' they are given in a story to carry out. One god can be 'over' or 'under' another god in a hierarchy, but then both 'rule', the one over the other - perhaps in a 'family' of gods, or after one god has 'defeated' another in a battle between their two 'peoples'. Gods always stand 'upright'—dominant—even if they are subordinated by another god or have endured defeat by him.

One reason for this inflexibility is the gods' association with the stars. Things on earth change, but stars do not change. The first theologies developed in the Middle East, which has predominantly a dry climate—ideal for stargazing and the development of a surprisingly expert astronomy—were considered identical and interchangeable. Hercules was a 'hero', and for his outstanding accomplishments at his death he was lifted up as a constellation. There was much cultural prestige associated with making more accurate predictions about the location and movements of the stars—predicting eclipses and the like—as with the three 'wise men' who come from the East seeking news about a new 'King of the Jews', because they have 'seen his star' in the East. Stars don't change, and compared to us, gods do not change. In the ancient world the 'lower' attends and obeys the 'higher'; the 'higher' never inclines, stoops or bows to the lower. Whatever else happens, this stays the same.

The chief thing people noticed about Jesus as a candidate to be the 'Messiah' or 'Anointed One' (new 'Moses' who would restore Israel) was that he had been killed—in fact, he was executed. This was not an auspicious beginning for a theology. Almost the whole of 'Christian Theology' came out of the paradoxical claim that in Christ, 'God suffered'. For the ancient mentality this doesn't make sense. That's not what gods are for. They are for something, but that's not it. They are for triumph and victory, not for defeat. Against ancient assumptions, this was worse than a blasphemy, it was virtually a contradiction in terms.

Plausibly, the creator would have to prepare for the eventuality that at least a certain percentage of creation would decline or reject the invitation to a proper relationship with its creator (most likely almost everyone at different times). If creatures are spread out in time and can 'repent' of earlier mistakes, this creates narrative 'room' for a rescue mission by the Father to offer such a 'second' decision, after an appropriate experience of the consequences of declining the first.

This could plausibly produce as well as make acceptable the 'scandal' of a 'suffering god' in the career, death and resurrection of Jesus. Thereby the Christian God is not limited to 'triumphing' or 'ruling', that defines and exhausts the classical theistic repertoire. The Judaeo-Christian God is bent, concave or 'pregnant' with the Christ, the adequate 'mirror' of the initial divine nature with which God falls in love, but this time with the capacity and willingness to agency to demonstrate this supra-classical divine goodness against a new background or on a new stage after the initial (partial) negative reception by free creation. Jesus is like the bound Isaac whom Abraham takes out for the all-important sacrifice, as willing to carry out God's own mission for him in a later or subsequent phase; it is 'god-himself'-in-mission—being consistent with himself in a new extension prompted by unusual circumstances created by the initial (negative) reception as a not-surprising consequence of the gift of freedom. Christ is that part of God's self willing to go out in the mission of rescuing those who can be rescued, at the price of God's demonstrating the extent of his goodness through his willingness to engage in the unanticipated and 'un-divine activity' of suffering in order to forestall and pre-empt a final human rejection, to keep open the possibility of redemption for those willing to turn back and be 'reconstituted' by a second 'imprint' of their divine source, this time in an act of conscious repentance and redemption. This is the extraordinary, non-classical act on God's part. Prometheus brought fire down from heaven, which was a great blessing. Christ goes further; he offers us the permanent possibility of arguing that our earlier (guilty) self was in fact not our 'true' self—who as it happens, is here present. Who would not accept a judicial process with such generous rules? So this is why, where and how suffering enters into the Christian divine constitution—holding open the initial offer of 'salvation' and relation with God even after its initial rejection.

Judaism of course demurred and eventually declined to accept Jesus as the Messiah, which means it declined to include suffering as a key part of God's nature. He wasn't the kind of messiah they were looking for. They remained, for the most part, wedded to the 'classical' conventions of divine goodness—might, power, lordship, strength and victory. God leads and dictates, the people hear and obey. God shows patience with his wayward and recalcitrant people, but this is limited and punished with repeated chastisements—floods, defeat, exile. Judaism never abandoned its covert ambition to become 'a great power'—similar to God in his 'classical' dress. We are so used to hearing Judaism list its 'woes' that we forget how often it interpreted its privileged status as the recipient of a 'unique covenant' with God , that we understate or overlook how often Israel interpreted this covenant as placing front and center God's promise to make Israel a 'great nation'—impressive in the same ways as the other 'great nations' of the day—Egypt, Babylon, etc.—in fact, the supreme state towards which all the other nations of the world would one day come 'streaming'. This was unrealistic megalomania on Israel's part. There was no way Israel could compete with the resources of the Nile River or the Tigris-Euphrates complex. The Old Testament regularly inflates Israel's modest size and regional success. In its various defeats and exiles, on the other hand, we see Israel as a dependent 'buffer' between empires east and west, constantly under pressure to enter into dangerous coalitions on pain of disappearing altogether. Yet Israel loved to fantasize that God loved Israel so uniquely that he would lift her up and make her the equal of such mighty powers!

In the light of day, however, the fantasy it would not abandon voluntarily, it soon lost involuntarily. After its several wars with Rome, Israel lost king and land; the Law alone remained as a legacy—much of it pertaining to a no longer existent temple. Christianity, during its formative period, could not entertain such a pipe dream, so this temptation was removed. Christ rode into Jerusalem on a prophetic donkey rather than a Davidic stallion. He did come to 'restore the kingdom of Israel', but in a sense different from the way the majority imagined. When he ultimately received a crown, it would be a crown of thorns. For the Jews the 'great deed of God' on behalf of the Jewish people was Moses' drowning of Pharaoh's army at the Red Sea. That is how we are 'saved'. For the Christians, it is Christ's sacrifice on the cross.

Jesus was distinctive and shocking in calling the Jewish God 'my Father', and replaced the edifice of covenant and temple law with parables that called people to personal transformation, rather than fixed adherence to an external standard, that was often difficult to discover. There was a 'downscaling' of religious ambitions from the national to the personal, an internalization and inversion of external legal emphases to what meets the other's need. Jesus did not dwell upon status or ceremony; he scrapped the covenant as a political document, substituting a personal relationship in prayer for its codicils and requirements, and sought healing and equality rather than victory and pre-eminence as signs of God's presence and concern. One should be ready to inconvenience oneself to rectify a situation or raise a burden, rather than file a claim for religio-cultural-historical recognition.

The resurrected Jesus is the daring Christian replacement for the desecrated and destroyed post-70 Jewish Temple. He carries out the principal functions of the latter, as a continuous seat of victory over our enemy the devil and by being the transforming and divinizing presence of God in our midst. He is now paradoxically an eternal human Temple who will suffer and be defeated no longer, an eternal high priest who continuously generates and executes acceptable worship. He is a new link between heaven and earth who thereby testifies and guarantees that the two orders will never again rip apart. By deferring to the Father through his apparently definitive 'defeat', he has paradoxically achieved the only effective and indestructible form of human victory. In this sense he is the longed for 'Messiah' who restores the fortunes of Israel.

Chapter 9

Clawing Our Way Back; Towards an Ever-Deeper Intervention

'Intervention' is a term used in psychological circles for a treatment modality where a family member's behavior has become sufficiently a matter of concern—either harmful, dangerous or shameful, and over a sufficiently long period of time during which other traditional, more modest or conventional modes of correction have been tried, but without success. What is distinctive about an intervention is that there is typically a distortion of vision in the individual engaging in misconduct such that he/she can justify the questionable behavior by mis-describing it as less serious than it might appear to another. This strategy of escape or evasion is taken away by having multiple family members or friends around the individual at the meeting such that they may correct him/her by saying, 'No, I was there, and at that time you did such-and-such,' or 'you said such-and-such', such that there is no possibility of denying it.

There is typically an element of arrogance or denial in the individual whose behavior is under scrutiny, and this correction by a family member or friend who cannot be intimidated into silence, collusion or cowardice constitutes a second painful experience of having his/her self-serving excuse or distortion of their behavior trampled, torn away and exposed as a self-serving lie by an individual who would prefer to pass himself off as an honest and possibly superior person. The mood and spirit of the meeting remains calm; no one raises their voice. But the individual at the center has no place to hide; his/her behavior is exposed to their entire family group and becomes a subject matter that can be discussed by all. No one is 'in charge' or passes final judgment. There is no single 'authority figure' against whose concluding evaluation the individual might rally in objection. The element of shame or embarrassment is an attack upon this second character flaw of mistaken or misplaced pride, a hidden or deeper attitude that, it is implied, should change along with the external behavior that is the surface or initial object of comment. It thus takes psychic strength, or requires psychic growth, to undergo an 'intervention'. Indeed, that is its purpose.

Consequences of bullying, inappropriate treatment, insult or injury by another are complex, but not difficult to disentangle. When we feel we have become an innocent victim to someone else's aggression or excessive use of power—and that this is more than a 'one-off' incident, but now more like a permanent aspect of our situation or characteristic of our condition that we cannot change—we not infrequently attempt to re-achieve or restore a sense of power or agency by finding a victim whom WE can bully, beat up or demean in our turn. Although such behavior is as unjust and inappropriate as in the first instance, it brings about an at least partial restoration of our self-esteem because we thereby demonstrate that there is at least one person over whom we DO have power. We are thus not only a victim or powerless, but equally powerful, or a bully in our turn. Although this may not be the best or most mature way of dealing with the psychological discomfort caused by the first situation—perhaps by confronting the bully threatening us and making him back down or modify his behavior—it does achieve partial restoration of status, agency and respect. We have at least taken our place in the 'pecking order', rather than lying prostrate and embarrassed at the bottom.

An 'equality' of justice—or rather, 'injustice' - is thereby re-established, spread down the line, so that all are treated equally badly. However, everyone also has at least some partial or minimal 'victory'. This may be the best way of dealing with a bad situation—where there is no 'just' authority at the top, whom we may appeal to. We may have to accept this until something better comes along. However, when we are honest we must admit that society itself is injured by such a 'solution', since the fellow-feeling and camaraderie we should feel towards everyone in our society is broken; instead, we evaluate each other coldly as potential victims. Habitual criminals in the lower socio-economic echelons have achieved a near-complete detachment from the people around them, including family members and neighbors - everyone they do not fear as more 'powerful' than themselves. However, the aim of socialization should be to strengthen and extend the bonds of fellow-feeling and concern, rather than reduce these to almost nothing.

In a society where there are more than one social or ethnic group, not infrequently one or the other feels themselves to be 'second-class' citizens and improperly deprived of the 'fellow-feeling' of others—and that they have a right to reciprocate. It is thus not uncommon for entire cultures to engage in such distortions and consequent behavior, when they find themselves in a permanently inferior or subordinate position with regard to another culture and with no possibility of reversing or evening the relationship. For example, through modern biblical criticism many scholars have come to the conclusion that Israel found itself in such a position with regard to the dominant cultures surrounding them that had the advantage of more substantial or impressive natural resources, chiefly Egypt and Babylon. Exposed to Hellenistic culture after the foundation of the city of Alexandria just beyond its southern border, Jews could not escape exposure to the cultural riches in history, literature, drama and philosophy that Greek education afforded, and in particular to the 'national epic', in which the gods themselves participated, that produced Greek identity and its Hellenistic mentality, cultivated by esteemed poets and presented on musical evenings by noble hosts for honored guests, as with Homer's *Aeneid* and *Odyssey*. Inevitably the question of a reciprocal Jewish 'national epic' sprang up, and here Jews were expeditious in filling the vacuum. They had ample material on hand—scribal histories from the northern and southern kingdoms, records and teachings of various prophetic schools who had ministered to and encouraged Israel after the surprising destruction of Solomon's Temple and the beginning of the 'Babylonian Exile', folk tales from the earlier 'judges', etc. This 'national epic' became the 'Old Testament' for Christians—but it requires some corrections. First of all, Abraham and Moses were legendary fictions, necessary to account for movements of the Jews into Canaan, and between Egypt and Canaan, when in fact such large movements never took place. Secondly, the monotheist Jewish theology came late, possibly in Babylon or as a borrowing from the Egyptian pharaoh Akhenaten, or even as an early reaction within Neo-Platonism, as a way of increasing the ethereal, asexual 'spirituality' of their God over material divinities. As the Israeli archaeologist Zeev Herzog has set this challenge: '(T)he Israelites were never in Egypt, did not wander in the desert, did not conquer the land in a military campaign, and did not pass it on to the twelve tribes of Israel. Perhaps even harder to swallow is the fact that the united monarchy of David and Solomon, which is described by the Bible as a regional power, was at most a small tribal kingdom. And it will come as an unpleasant shock to many that the God of Israel, Jehovah, had a female consort and that the early Israelite religion adopted monotheism only in the waning period of the monarchy and not at Mount Sinai.' (quoted in *The Jews and the Bible,* by Jean-Christophe Attias, Stanford UP, 2014, pp. 149-50). If you cannot raise the bridge, lower the river. If you don't dare insult the gods of your masters, praise the 'spirituality' of your own god and criticize others for not living up to an equal standard. Monotheism came at the end of Jewish development, not at its beginning. It barely preceded Jesus.

Another factor inhibiting correct appraisal of a person or institution we cannot escape is an attitude of approval, affection or respect that has been inculcated over centuries and been culturally mandatory as long as anyone can remember. In such circumstances, critical examination or the discarding of such an attitude can lead to considerable psychological upheaval and even social disorder. An inhibiting factor in the latter situation is the unpopularity with which we expect our modification to be received. A recent example is the reaction of some political analysts and historical scholars to the official charge that Lee Harvey Oswald was the lone gunman of President John F. Kennedy in 1963. To oppose this 'official' interpretation, one must be willing to entertain the hypothesis of a deep and widespread conspiracy, made up not just of the F.B.I. who investigated the killing on site, but J. Edgar Hoover as its head, the C. I. A., military chiefs together with the new president Lyndon Johnson and the members of the Warren Commission who later investigated the assassination. Nevertheless, a not-inconsiderable number of professional investigators and scholars who have come at this tragedy with an open mind have discovered a surprising number of anomalies in the official transcription of the attack and handling of the resulting corpse. The supposition is that Kennedy was not as ideologically rigid or intellectually committed to a strict anti-communism as others in the U. S. military and government establishment. He was 'soft' on Fidel Castro in Cuba and looking for a way to free the United States from the conflict in Vietnam that looked more like a cultural liberation movement. Supposedly Kennedy's critics wanted a return to a post-World War II cold-war opposition. They were not ready to 'move on' to a more flexible discussion.

To entertain this hypothesis, however, one must be psychologically ready to reconsider one's opinion not only of J. Edgar Hoover and the other leaders of government, but also of the history and integrity of the basic institutions of American government, against which such an accusation had never before been laid. Whatever the logical 'weight' of the contrary evidence, the psychological habit of loyalty to the elected regime coming out of the Second World War was such as to make it difficult to take this proposal seriously. The debate broke into a scattered discussion by acknowledged 'hot-heads' and government apologists that left the basic issues unresolved and the general public at sea as to what intelligently could be said at this comparatively late date on the affair. Thus the matter rests.

A similar confused scholarly opinion today attends the historical reliability of the Jewish scriptures or the attempt to take them 'literally'. Can they be trusted to say what they appear to say, or are they rather a late composition trying to cobble together a 'national epic' that could stand with and compete against such compositions as the 'great nations' of the region told about themselves, and paraded before the 'outside' world as well? What scholarly attitude should the intelligent reader take towards this body of texts, about which the received attitude is now divided even among professionals?

In this situation, 'intervention' may offer us a way to get a handle on prayer. Prayer may be looked upon as a way of doing an 'intervention' for and on yourself—with yourself taking all the roles! The ground for this is that intervention as a psychological device concerns rooting out self-deception - self-deception is impossible in authentic prayer. Prayer is thus the search for a deeper intervention than we normally pursue or aim at—a way to push ourselves towards our 'best' selves. We can call ourselves out, because we know the ways by which we typically shield ourselves from a deeper responsibility; we can also comfort ourselves when we need help and aid from this other direction. All this is in support of the fundamental human project of living closer to—what? Why, simply to the most important thing we could call an 'intervention'.